PRAISE FOR A SONG FOR THE WORLD

"When inspired genius is willing to renounce ease and glory for the sake of something greater, the impact is huge. This is the lesson of the incredible Colwell/Allen story. My eyes and ears are witness to the joy and hope that Herb Allen and the Colwell Brothers triggered in country after country. The words of their songs came from seeing into the heart of humanity, and I think they got their music from a divine source. I thank God for them, and I thank them for adding memorably to my stock of faith and hope."

Rajmohan Gandhi
Grandson of Mahatma Gandhi
Visiting professor, South Asian and Middle Eastern Studies
University of Illinois at Urbana-Champaign

"Many who made a difference in global history have gone unsung, lost in the scope of big players on the big stages. But the wonderful Colwell Brothers and Herb Allen have left a lasting legacy through their songs, lyrics, and the lives of over 20,000 Up with People students around the world. They are writers for all times and all seasons and they have touched the hearts of millions."

Tom Sullivan
Singer, actor, author

"We all treasure those who have positively influenced our lives, and I count Herb Allen and the Colwells among my most valuable inspirations. But as completely as I thought I was aware of their kaleidoscopic pasts, this book has opened my eyes to travels, adventures, and relationships I could never have dreamed they experienced. Up with People's appearances on the Super Bowl halftime shows changed the genre forever, and directing them was a highlight of my network television career. *A Song for the World* is a great reference work for those who aspire to live life to the fullest."

John Gonzalez
Director, NBC Sports and the NFL Network

"I thought I knew these guys until I read this book. What an adventure life has taken them on! Even if you've never heard of the Colwells, Herb Allen, or Up with People, the musical journey they have had makes for incredible reading. Their music has influenced the lives of millions of people, including me. I now know where their inspiration came from!"

David Grossman
Executive vice president
National Academy of Recording Arts & Sciences (The Grammys)

"Steve, Paul, and Ralph Colwell and Herb Allen broke with orthodoxy and set out to lift the spirit of the human family. Their legacy lives in the thousands and thousands who have caught their fervor. Over the past forty years I have seen them in action in some of the most unbelievable places and situations. They have never failed to capture their audience and inspire them to make a difference in their community and country. It is still 'an unfinished world,' and perhaps their story can be a textbook for all who still dream that their lives can play a part in building a more peaceful future. A. W. E. O'Shaughnessy in his poem 'Ode' might well have been describing these modern troubadours:

We are the music makers and we are the dreamers of dreams....
Yet we are the movers and shakers of the world forever, it seems.

"We salute their courage and selfless service to humanity."

J. Blanton Belk
Founder and chairman emeritus, Up with People

"They were the most effective ambassadors during their time in the Congo. Their message was straight, simple and fun, and not preaching."

Dr. William T. Close
Chief medical doctor for the Congolese National Army
Personal physician to Congolese President Mobutu
Author of Ebola

"Anyone who feels hopeless about the present state of the world should pick up a copy of *A Song for the World*. In it, Frank McGee tells the deeply inspiring story of four men who quietly and gently set out to change the world and, in the process, sparked one of the great youth movements of all time: Up with People. I don't know what's most extraordinary about the Colwell Brothers and Herb Allen: their work around the world in the service of peace, their body of unforgettable music, their legacy as youth leaders, or the fact that through it all they have remained so remarkably humble. *A Song for the World* is a must-read for anyone who dreams of making the world a better place."

Mark Glubke
Senior editor, Back Stage Books

"The Colwell Brothers and Herb Allen believed they could change the world and impact society. As an alumna of Up with People, I saw firsthand the difference the program made in individual lives and communities and young cast members developing into leaders. The experience confirmed my dedication to a life of public service. The Center for Public Leadership at Harvard's Kennedy School of Government is another example of a place filled with young people from across the world who want to make a positive difference. The Colwell Brothers and Herb Allen are living examples of how individuals with an idea, determination, and passion can serve the greater good. They are truly an inspiration to public servants, social activists, and those of us at the Kennedy School."

Betsy Myers
Executive director, Center for Public Leadership
John F. Kennedy School of Government, Harvard University

"*A Song for the World* is a remarkable story of courage, commitment, vision, and learning."

W. Timothy Gallwey
Author, The Inner Game of Tennis

"I have known the Colwell Brothers and Herb Allen for over fifty years and observed their work in many countries. With Hollywood and musical stardom beckoning in the 1950s, they chose instead to become part of a great endeavor to shift the whole world Godward, turning enemies into friends. This involved much sacrifice: ceaseless travel, rough living conditions, and sensitive research into different cultures and countries, all without thought of financial reward. Out of this sacrifice came great creativity. They gave an image of America that millions responded to. They richly deserve the title of musical diplomats. Frank McGee has done a great service in making their extraordinary life stories available to all."

Archie Mackenzie
Retired British ambassador
Participant in the creation of the United Nations

"They've been called the musical founders of Up with People, and that is how they will go down in history. Yet the Colwell Brothers and Herb Allen have contributed much more than the music. They have been the moral compass of the organization. More than anyone else, they represent the integrity, values, sincerity, and humility of what Up with People stands for. Period."

Tommy Spaulding
President and CEO, Up with People, Inc.

"This excellent book on the Colwell Brothers and Herb Allen's adventures is absorbing reading from start to finish. Their creative outpouring is astounding and reflects not only their extraordinary gifts, but also their commitment to service, their all-outness, and their genuine humility. They represented across the world the very best of America, and the world is better off for all they did."

Richard Ruffin
Former executive director
Moral Re-Armament/Initiatives of Change

"To say people have an 'aura' may sound quirky, but some are hard to describe any other way. The Colwell Brothers and Herb Allen have this impact. They weren't driven by monetary reward or fame; their goal was to use their God-given talents for the betterment of others, the finding of new talent, and the nurturing and development of each one, not restricted to musical skill. It was all about 'people.' These four mean more to me than I can express in words. This book is long overdue."

David Mackay
British record producer

"*A Song for the World* is truly an awe-inspiring view into the lives of four men whose vision for a better world affected people from all walks of life in scores of countries through the ultimate language of music."

Jill C. Johnson
Former director of creative development
American Society of Composers, Authors, and Publishers (ASCAP)

A SONG FOR THE WORLD

Colwell Brothers

Steve Paul Ralph

Herb Allen

Frank Miller

A SONG

The Amazing Story of
The Colwell Brothers and
Herb Allen: Musical Diplomats

FOR THE
WORLD

How Vision, Creativity, and Commitment Sparked the
Up with People Phenomenon

FRANK MCGEE

MANY ROADS
PUBLISHING

SANTA BARBARA, CALIFORNIA

Many Roads Publishing
2069 Las Canoas Road, Santa Barbara, CA 93105
(805) 898-3677 • (800) 679-6374 • Fax (805) 898-3679
www.manyroadspublishing.com • info@manyroadspublishing.com

Publisher's Cataloging-In-Publication
McGee, Frank.
   A song for the world : how vision, creativity, and commitment
sparked the Up With People phenomenon / Frank McGee. -- 1st ed.
-- Santa Barbara, Calif. : Many Roads Publishing, 2007.

   p. ; cm.
   ISBN-13: 978-0-9787948-1-1
   978-0-9787948-0-4 (pbk.)
   ISBN-10: 0-9787948-1-8
   0-9787948-0-X (pbk.)
   "The amazing story of the Colwell Brothers and Herb Allen :
musical diplomats."

   1. Up with People (Organization) 2. Allen, Herb. 3. Colwell
Brothers. 4. Vocal groups--United States--History. 5. Leadership.
   I. Title.

ML421.U6 M33 2007   2006934699
782.00973--dc22

Printed and bound in the United States of America on acid-free paper.

Book Consultant: Ellen Reid
Book cover and interior design: Patricia Bacall
Editor: Melanie Rigney
Photographers and resources:
David Channer, Robert J. Fleming, Arthur Strong, Richard Hadden, Michael Blundell,
Albert H. Ely, Jurg Kobler, Hans Magnus, Al Cook, the Colwell Brothers and families, the Herb Allen family, Charles Piguet, Eric Junod, Scott McGee, Leena Liukkonen-Suomaa, David Allen, Frank McGee, Stewart Lancaster, Bert Demmers, Wendy Alexander, Rachel Paul, Ron Roberts, Jerry von Teuber, Tom Wilkes, David Beal, Malcolm Roberts, Hideo Nakajima, Peter Sisam, Pace Publications, IOC (MRA) archives, Up with People archives, Brian Boobyer, and Van Wishard.
Cover: The Colwell Brothers and Herb Allen in the spotlight at the 25th anniversary of Up with People, Denver, Colorado, 1990.

"Music is the only thing which all nations, all ages, all ranks, and both sexes do equally well. It is sooner or later the great world bond."

Edward Thring
Headmaster, Uppingham School, Rutland, England, 1862

This book is dedicated to the Colwell Brothers' and Herb Allen's parents,
Paul and True Colwell, and Herb and Dot Allen,
who invested their treasure in a better world.

ACKNOWLEDGMENTS

First and foremost, to publisher John Ruffin, whose passion for the story of Herb Allen and the Colwell Brothers has been demonstrated in countless hours, endless patience, and unlimited encouragement.

To Jack Hipps and Hans Magnus, whose journals of historic Up with People tours lent eyewitness presence to the chapters on China and the USSR.

To Debbie Colwell, for the chronology of a global odyssey.

To Alice Chaffee, for wise and generous editorial and historical input.

To Morris Martin, Robert Fleming, Stewart Lancaster, David Allen and Malcolm Roberts for editorial review.

To the many Colwell/Allen friends and fans from around the world for stories and pictures.

And to Ellen Reid, our Book Shepherd, and her exceptional team: book cover and interior designer Patricia Bacall, copywriter Laren Bright, and copy editor Melanie Rigney, who have worked creatively and tirelessly to produce A Song for the World.

Table of Contents

FOREWORD

The Colwell Brothers and Herb Allen had something important for all to hear, particularly the generations of young people who were confronted with a changing and often confusing world. It was a message of hope, of peace, of excitement, and of challenge that penetrated the hearts and minds of us all, told in a language the world could intimately understand, interpreted through music and song.

Those early days of Up with People took them from the exuberance of the Super Bowl, through the closed thresholds of China, the unrest in Africa, the strife in Northern Ireland, and from these four adventurers came the words of songs such as "Where the Roads Come Together," "Give the Children Back Their Childhood," and the challenge from the captain in "Moon Rider" "...to cross the next frontier." And we can never forget the inspiration from "Up, up with people."

After I returned from my voyage to the moon on Apollo 17, I often described my impressions of seeing the earth from a quarter million miles away as a world without any borders and without any fighting. Steve, Paul, Ralph, and Herb were in the forefront of those who dedicated their lives to the hope of making that vision a reality. This book tells their story in dramatic detail, from Hollywood to the dusty roads of India, revolution in the Congo, the struggle for independence in Cyprus and beyond.

This is a story that resonates today with young and old who are looking for a way to make a meaningful contribution to world peace. It is real-life experience from the hearts and souls of the Colwell Brothers and Allen—the places they've been, the people they've met, and the memories indelibly etched in their minds—and it's as relevant today as it was in the twentieth century.

May this story be heard around the world!

Captain Eugene A. Cernan, USN (Ret),
Apollo 17 commander and author of *The Last Man on the Moon*

"Where the Roads Come Together"
Paul Colwell and Herb Allen

None of us is born the same,
We don't know why
It's the way we came,
Every heart beats a little differently,
Each soul is free to find its way,
Like a river that winds its way to the sea.

For life is a journey,
And there are many roads beneath the sky,
And there are many good people
Who don't see eye to eye.

Not everyone can sing your tune,
From where he stands there's another view,
With every turn we're learning more,
And perhaps we'll find that the walls we build
Are only, are only in the mind.

> *There are many roads to go,*
> *And they go by many names.*
> *They don't all go the same way,*
> *But they get there all the same.*
> *And I have a feelin'*
> *That we'll meet some day*
> *Where the roads come together*
> *Up the way.*

INTO THE VENTURE

There's no contesting the fact that Steve, Paul, and Ralph Colwell and Herb Allen experienced decades of unparalleled adventure. As musicians, they toured in the farthest corners of the world, performing from the White House to the Super Bowl, from Watts to Carnegie Hall. Yet millions who have seen them know little or nothing of the astounding story of their lives.

The Colwells, city boys from San Marino, California, strummed and sang their way onto bluegrass and country stages at ages fourteen, twelve, and ten. They were picked up as performers by radio and TV stations in the Midwest and startled the "old boys" by winning the Renfro Valley Hillbilly Band Contest in Kentucky. Soon they were regulars on radio and TV programs in Southern California, and are said to have been the youngest trio under contract with a major label, Columbia Records.

Herb Allen was a child prodigy. He conducted the Seattle Baby Orchestra at age four, became an accomplished keyboard player and percussionist, and had his own dance band in high school. He was a student of classical piano and was accepted by the prestigious Oberlin School of Music.

After high school graduation, Allen launched into an adventure that would catapult him into the theaters of post-World War II Europe. He was young, the Colwell Brothers even younger, and the eyes of the world were on their generation. In the decade that followed, through an extraordinary mix of decision, courage, and commitment, the world became their stage.

The Colwells and Allen preceded the baby boomer generation by ten to twenty years. They were not old enough to fight in World War II and were too old to be drafted for the Vietnam War. (The fourth Colwell brother, Ted, eight years younger than Ralph, served in Vietnam.) Allen was called up during the Korean War, but received a deferment. Steve, Paul, Ralph, and Herb were part of the so-called "quiet generation," not expected to stir things up very much. As it turned out, they were anything but quiet.

In the '40s and '50s, they left careers, sweethearts, and family behind and set sail for the far corners of the world. Their adventures and experiences uniquely prepared them to ride the whirlwind of the 1960s.

Youth dominated the headlines of the sixties with marches, sit-ins, protests, and great new music. No one over thirty could be trusted. Traditions and mores that had bound society for centuries were shaking loose. American youth were gripped by a new idealism, much of it inspired by John Kennedy's challenge, "Ask not what your country can do for you; ask what you can do for your country." This new idealism drew thousands of young people to take up the challenge of Modernizing America, the theme of mid-decade student leadership conferences at Michigan's Mackinac Island where Up with People was born.

The Colwells and Allen arrived at the first Michigan conference in 1964 after working in Europe, Asia, Africa, the Americas, and Australia for more than a decade. They had played and sung in areas of tension and crisis in dozens of countries. No one at the conference was aware of how much sweat, grit, fatigue, and sacrifice had gone into those years. This is the story of their roots, of the passion and dedication behind the birth of Up with People.

Paul and Ralph Colwell, Herb Allen, David Mackay

"200 Years and Just a Baby"

200 years and just a baby,
200 years and just a child,
Growing like weed
Kinda rough, kinda wild,
Someday she's going to be quite a lady,
Yeah, she's 200 years and just a baby.

China's been around five thousand years,
Egypt's been here four,
The Greeks some thirty centuries,
And the British aren't quite sure.
The Aussies couldn't tell you
'Cause they forgot to keep the score,
The Swiss are seven hundred
And the Romans ain't no more.

The tide rolls over Plymouth Rock,
The moon turns in its dust,
The swords of Appomattox and Little Big Horn
Have turned to rust.
She's sipped the wine of victory,
Felt the pain of being burned.
But that's all right 'cause nothing's lost
As long as something's learned.

Super Bowl X: Inventing the Halftime Spectacular

O n a cool desert evening in the fall of 1974, the telephone rang in the suburban Tucson home of Steve and Lynn Colwell.

"Hello, this is Pete Rozelle," said the voice.

Steve's heart skipped a beat.

"Oh, hello, Mr. Rozelle. Good evening." Rozelle was commissioner of the National Football League and a friend of Lynn's father, Herb Hutner, a prominent Los Angeles businessman.

Rozelle was calling to invite Up with People to produce the halftime show for Super Bowl X in 1976, America's bicentennial year. The game would be played in Miami's Orange Bowl and globally televised. Rozelle said Lynn's father had suggested Up with People's international casts could give a new dimension to the event. Steve assured him he'd have an answer soon and the call ended.

Steve, typically undemonstrative, turned to his wife with a grin as broad as his face.

"Well, what do you know? Pete Rozelle wants us to create a halftime show for the Super Bowl!"

Steve and his brothers, Paul and Ralph, along with Herb Allen, had sparked the creation of the Up with People show a decade earlier. "But we'd never dreamed of anything like this happening. It was simply beyond our imaginations," Steve said.

The Colwells themselves defied imagination. They were radio, TV, and recording artists in their teens. And from the early 1950s, with their friend and collaborator, Herb Allen, they worked in volunteer nation-building efforts and played to kings and commoners literally everywhere.

Steve, the oldest, had a guileless face with eyes that seemed to smile perpetually beneath an always-neat head of red-brown hair. Ralph, the youngest, not only

"Well, what do you know? Pete Rozelle wants us to create a halftime show for the Super Bowl!"

In the mid '60s, the Colwells and Allen had simply wanted to create a showcase for the talents of youth at student leadership conferences on Mackinac Island in Michigan. They knew they'd provide entertainment for the locals and summer visitors, but no one had seen further than that.

looked the junior but would maintain his youthful appearance for decades. Paul's face had an angularity that made him the most memorable of the three. All three, through charm, talent, or just plain good luck, seemed able to walk through any door and find a welcome.

Herb Allen was shorter and muscular, with a winsome smile. A virtuoso xylophonist, he would astound listeners with the velocity of "The Flight of the Bumble Bee." As a skilled concert pianist, no chord or span seemed beyond the reach of his seemingly too-short fingers and hands. He possessed an inexhaustible sense of humor, and was hopelessly addicted to puns.

In the mid '60s, the Colwells and Allen had simply wanted to create a showcase for the talents of youth at student leadership conferences on Mackinac Island in Michigan. They knew they'd provide entertainment for the locals and summer visitors, but no one had seen further than that.

At the 1964 gathering, bolstered by the energy and enthusiasm of the students, the program organizers had set up a giant tent on an athletic field for Sing Out evenings after the conference sessions. Talent was abundant. A seaworthy motorized gravel barge was located and turned into a kind of showboat that could power itself from marina to marina around the Great Lakes, and the students sang from their floating stage to crowds who gathered at the docksides.

In 1965 during a three-day road trip to the conference from Arizona, Paul and Ralph started writing a song they titled "Up with People." Steve said later, "Hey, I drove the car! Doesn't that count?" The new song became the finale for the '65 production.

That summer, Henry Cass, a leading British producer/director, flew in from London and helped the Colwells and Allen turn a series of performances into a full-fledged musical. The show became an overnight sensation and late that summer toured the Northeast. Another barge was procured, and in Martha's Vineyard and other historic settings around Cape Cod, thousands streamed to the harbors to see and hear the innovative demonstration of youth.

Those were the years when young people across the world were shaking society, not only with sit-ins and rallies, but also with activism and a new idealism that found its voice in music. That idealism splintered into a plethora of forms and expressions, far beyond the "sex, drugs, and rock 'n' roll" clichés. It was the beginning of the Peace Corps, and it included the youth at the Michigan conferences who were embracing the challenge of "Modernizing America." There was much in society that needed to be remedied, and at a time of "Down with this," and "Down with that," the idea of "Up with People" resonated.

David Allen (no relation to Herb), a talented songwriter, wrote about the show in *Up with People's Musical Inheritance* (2000): "They sensed they had created a promising musical review. Yet none could foresee that *Sing Out '65*, soon to be renamed Up with People, was destined within a year to become a runaway hit on three continents. Nor did any of them dream that, from its opening performance on August 7 in Stamford, Connecticut the show would be in continuous production for the next thirty-four years, making it one of the longest running musical productions in America, and possibly the world, in the 20th century."

By the time Pete Rozelle telephoned in 1974, Paul Colwell was creative director, Ralph was production director, Steve was director of admissions, and Herb Allen was music director of a program that annually was taking more than seven hundred college-age students in multiple casts on a one-year tour to stage the production and learn about themselves and the world.

Steve telephoned four people that night: Paul, Ralph, Herb, and Blanton Belk. Belk, a naval officer in World War II, had chaired the student leadership conferences. When Up with People incorporated in 1968 as a nonprofit educational company, he became its president. A meeting was called for the next morning.

Ralph recognized that a radically new Super Bowl halftime concept was called for. Typically, marching bands played and created formations, and sometimes floats appeared. "We were not a marching band and obviously needed to invent an entirely different kind of production," he recalled.

To get a handle on what lay ahead, Ralph and Steve flew to New Orleans in January 1975 to watch Super Bowl IX. The halftime show was a tribute to Duke Ellington with Mercer Ellington and the Grambling University bands.

"The game was at the old Tulane University stadium, an iron relic from early in the century," Ralph said. "The halftime was not particularly memorable, but the size and scope of the event was huge. Producing a spectacular program that would showcase Up with People with a bicentennial theme seemed daunting, to say the least."

"We knew it would take exceptional creativity and imagination," Steve recalled.

There was much in society that needed to be remedied, and at a time of "Down with this," and "Down with that," the idea of "Up with People" resonated.

As it turned out, the initial imagination came from the National Football League. The NFL's technical manager enthused to Ralph in an early planning session, "My dream is to have musicians, singers, and dancers blanket the field with color."

A two-hundredth-birthday composition had already begun to germinate in Paul's mind from a thought of Ralph's: "Two hundred years and just a baby." The production team was soon in place. Herb Allen would conduct the cast and orchestra. Steve Rokowski, who had joined Up with People at age seventeen four years earlier, would be the technical director. And dancer/choreographer Lynne Morris, who arranged the dance corps for the *Dean Martin Show* and had just designed the Broadway musical *Mother Earth*, would create a completely new concept for the very first Super Bowl halftime spectacular.

Morris had become Up with People's choreographer in 1971. Highly regarded for her artistic brilliance, she had the skill to utilize large numbers of people in seamless movement on stages. Yet this was a stage beyond even her experience, so she contacted a young director of a championship drum and bugle corps to help her design the movement of hundreds of performers on a football field. Lynne and Ralph concluded they would need two stages: one at the midfield sideline for the musicians, and one at centerfield for the featured dancers.

What happened outside the Super Bowl was as dramatic as the show itself. Typically, Up with People casts toured half the year in North America and the other half overseas. But during the bicentennial "season," a performance schedule blanketing America was arranged. Nine casts with members from forty states and seventeen countries were on tour in the United States that year. Into that mix came the preparations for the Super Bowl.

"We divided the field into sections," choreographer Morris explained, "so that wherever they were, a cast could rehearse. It was like fitting puzzles together in different parts of the country and then coming to Miami to put all the little puzzles together into one great big one."

"We were attempting two revolutionary concepts," Ralph said. "One was to choreograph the free movement of four hundred performers using an entire football field; the second was to use super amplified sound to bring the power of the music to the stadium. The whole show would be without tape, nothing recorded."

Steve Rokowski described the challenges: "We had to fit everything into a fourteen-minute time slot and had exactly two and a half minutes at the start to put the entire cast and stages in place and set up a sound system with speakers powerful enough to reach people at the top of the arena. It was the first time equipment for live sound had been used in a halftime. We didn't want to put the show through the stadium's bull-horns." All this was breaking new ground for the Super Bowl, Rokowski said. "The NFL was as young at doing this as we were. We built the stages using the shells of their floats from the Orange Bowl Parade facility."

"From the start, our staffs worked with the NFL's top people, including Executive Director Don Weiss and Director of Special Events Jim Steig," Ralph said. "With the stress those executives lived under, including the negotiation of multimillion-dollar TV contracts, we weren't sure how they would regard our upstart organization. But they could not have been more supportive. They showed us great respect."

As the casts began rehearsing the program around the country, weather was proving to be a wild card.

"We were doing a lot of shows in school assemblies," recalled one member, "and when we could, we practiced on their athletic fields. The administrators were excited to help us prepare for the Super Bowl."

"And we were just as excited to learn about the weather predictions," said another from Costa Rica, who was experiencing her first Midwest winter. "We probably looked pretty strange to the people in one town, a hundred of us marching around in sync in a snowstorm." They could hardly wait to get to Florida.

Early in December, just weeks before the Super Bowl, a new element was added to the mix. Blanton Belk received a call from Pete Rozelle, who asked to have Up with People perform the national anthem. The anthem had always

Paul Colwell's theme song for the Super Bowl show grew from a title suggested by brother Ralph, "Two Hundreds Years and Just a Baby." Paul and his brothers, together with Herb Allen, wrote hundreds of songs for audiences large and small. The Super Bowl halftime show in America's bicentennial year would be their biggest audience ever, carried on television to an audience of over ninety million.

Dancer/chorographer Lynne Morris designed theatrical and TV productions from L.A. to Broadway. For Super Bowl X, she would create an entirely new concept for a Super Bowl halftime, utilizing four hundred singers and dancers on the stage of an entire football field. Up with People produced four halftime shows. Super Bowl XIV in 1980 (right) was held at the Rose Bowl in Pasadena, California.

kicked off the game, he said, but for the bicentennial year, it needed to be presented in a truly memorable way. Belk knew whom to call.

Tom Sullivan was then very much in the public eye, which might sound ironic, because Sullivan was blind. That didn't matter to him; since his youth, he had admitted to no limitations. He went to Harvard, was a skydiver, ran marathons, snow- and water-skied, and played golf. His book, *If You Could See What I Hear*, a *New York Times* best-seller, was about to be made into a movie. Tom had appeared scores of times on TV as a regular on *Good Morning America*, on *The Tonight Show Starring Johnny Carson*, and on programs from *Mork and Mindy* to *M.A.S.H.* In addition to all that, Sullivan had a magnificent voice.

"When Blanton called me about doing the national anthem," Sullivan recalled, "I said yes, but I don't know if I understood then the impact. This would be the first time the anthem was to be truly featured. I asked myself, 'Do I have the courage to let the human voice sound naked in an enormous place like that stadium, echoes and all?'

"Herb Allen and I had worked on many projects together, and I phoned him right away. I asked him to think about how we might do the anthem with 'just voices.' He got very excited about the idea and said, 'Call me in the morning.'

"It was a Friday, and he had paper and pencil ready. The anthem was originally written in the key of A, but we were going to do it in C. I told Herb I wanted to hit the fifth octave C at the end. 'You'll get a hernia!' he protested between laughs. Herb has perfect pitch and is a genius. We started on the arrangement, got so excited, and wrote the whole chart in twenty-five minutes. The only problem was that I wouldn't be able to get to Miami until the day before the game. I was really hot right then and was in the middle of producing my first album."

"In theory," reflected Ralph, "Miami had seemed the ideal place for outdoor rehearsals. But a major cold front pushed into the southern part of the state that week. What caused the most havoc with our schedule was that the NFL, which had not seen what we were doing or understood the scope of it, had given us no time for rehearsals in the stadium. We had to put the pieces from all over the country together on a high school field in Fort Lauderdale. We couldn't get into the Orange Bowl until the day before the game, and then only for a few hours. We were way beyond nervous."

Those limited hours were also the only chance for Sullivan and the cast to practice together, and until then, no one had heard the anthem as it would be performed.

"As soon as the rehearsal began," Tom recalled, "chills ran up and down my spine. 'This is my Olympics,' I thought. 'This is my chance at a gold medal!' That night I could hardly sleep."

Compounding the drama, the cast had to work around a Hollywood crew filming a segment of the movie *Black Sunday*. The thriller, which starred Robert Shaw and would include footage of the cast, was plotted around a terrorist attack in which a blimp loaded with deadly projectiles was programmed to explode above a stadium packed with unsuspecting Super Bowl fans.

"That night we had some terror attacks of our own," Ralph remembered. "I wandered around the motel complex where I stayed trying to find someone to talk with to get my mind off what was looming. The next day, we were supposed to perform on the world's biggest stage in front of eighty thousand people, and on TV to the largest audience on the planet. We had never anticipated a situation like this."

Herb's last thought before he went to bed was, "Can Tom really hit that high C?"

~

Game day dawned clear and cold. At first light, the smoky aroma of bacon wafted over the fleets of motor homes that had overnighted in the parking lots around the arena. The excitement was palpable: who would take home the coveted trophy of Super Bowl X, the Pittsburgh Steelers or the Dallas Cowboys?

But no one felt more tension than the Colwells, Allen, Sullivan, and the four hundred Up with People performers for whom this was not only the moment of the year, but very possibly of a lifetime.

Over breakfast in more than 230 homes peppered across Miami, host families were taking care of their young guests. Many, according to an unofficial survey taken later, included pancakes on the menu. Breakfast chatter centered on previous day's rehearsals, pivotal points of the day's show, and what the response of friends and families would be.

"I'd had nightmares," trumpeter Scott Dickey recalled, "about phoning Doc Severinsen (famed trumpeter and leader of the Tonight Show band) to ask how he liked the performance and being told he couldn't come to the phone because he was rolling around on the floor laughing."

Tom Sullivan would sing the National Anthem at the start of the game, without accompaniment. Sullivan was no stranger to pressure: he was frequently on television, skydived, played golf, ran marathons, snow- and water-skied. And he was blind. "This is my Olympics," he said to himself after his one rehearsal before the game. "This is my chance at a gold medal!"

In the stadium, Rokowski and his crew checked and double-checked the sound system and stages. The day was sunny and Miami-beautiful, although the post-cold front breeze was playing havoc with the microphones and TV commentators were already telling the world that if the wind freshened, it might blow an extra-point kick off course and even decide the outcome of the game.

The stadium was packed. The players had been introduced and, led by their superstar quarterbacks, the Steelers' Terry Bradshaw and the Cowboys' Roger Staubach, stood waiting for the opening ceremony to begin.

Twenty-year-old Scott Dickey, a trumpeter in Herb Allen's orchestra, was given a role he would never forget. "I was to be in the middle of the field with my horn, and all by myself play the first six notes of the national anthem. That might not sound too hard, but the arrangement was in C." The trumpet is a B-flat instrument, and the key of C challenges horn players.

"I'd had nightmares," Dickey recalled, "about phoning Doc Severinsen (famed trumpeter and leader of the *Tonight Show* band) to ask how he liked the performance and being told he couldn't come to the phone because he was rolling around on the floor laughing."

Yet Dickey felt he was prepared "until I got out there and found three television cameras looking up my nose!"

"I was a mass of nerves," Tom Sullivan said. "Herb hugged me and said, 'Tom, you can sing those notes.' There I was on the sideline as the announcer began, '…and now, our national anthem, sung by Tom Sullivan and the cast of Up with People!' And while he was saying that, Pete Rozelle had his hand on my shoulder and was saying in my ear, 'OK, young man, there are ninety million people out there—don't screw it up!' Big help. I walked out onto the field absolutely panicked. Scott's hands were shaking as he played the opening notes; I could hear it. When I hit the high C at the end, the crowd just seemed to explode. A girl from the cast took my arm to lead me off the field. My legs were jelly."

Coanchor Brent Musburger said to the TV audience, "I don't believe I have ever heard the anthem sung better. That was so strong."

"It was the musical highlight for my life," Sullivan said, "thanks to the magic of Herb Allen."

The kickoff immediately followed the anthem and the game proved to be a classic. Shortly before the halftime, the announcer's pregame prediction of wind affecting scoring was proven true as an attempted field goal sailed wide of the mark. Not a single Up with People cast member noticed it, however; concentration on the show was at its peak. Then the whistle blew for the end of the first half.

Almost as if a genie had snapped his fingers, in just 150 seconds the stages were in place, the musicians were positioned, and four hundred performers were spotted along the sidelines. TV coanchor Phyllis George, who had been Miss America 1971, introduced the show to the ninety million watching at home. Herb Allen gave the downbeat and the cast swarmed on to the field to the solid beat of "Up with People" in celebration of America's heritage. Next came Paul and Ralph's bicentennial song, "200 Years and Just a Baby."

The cast formed a giant "200," and then an enormous eagle. The announcer spoke of the people of other lands and the music and dance of America, as the field came alive with the charleston, the hustle, the Virginia reel, and the stomp. From "Country Roads" to "City of New Orleans," dance formations came and went. Elton John's "Philadelphia Freedom" triggered the image of an enormous Liberty Bell, followed by a field-spanning outline of the United States. Then the pace changed with "America the Beautiful" as a giant flower blossomed and multicolored streamers stretched out from the stage to the edges of the field. Then, as the shadow of the camera blimp crossed over the performers, thousands of balloons were released into the sky, and under crashing waves of exit music and audience applause, the cast and equipment vanished.

Musburger turned to Phyllis George and said, "You know, Phyllis, when you see and hear young people like that, you get a lot of confidence in the next two hundred years."

Decades later, a friend showed Ralph Colwell an Internet article about notable country music recordings. It identified the Detroit-born brothers as "Motor City bluegrass legends," citing their early Columbia Records releases. "They went missing in action," the author wrote. "Wonder what happened to them?"

If he only knew.

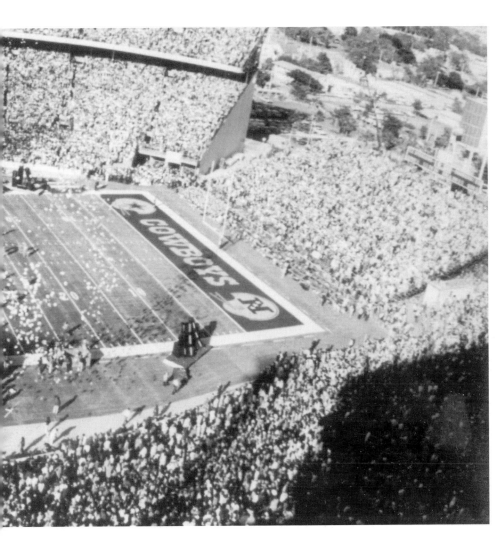

Up with People's performance at Super Bowl X launched the modern halftime spectacular. In the final number of the bicentennial show, banners streamed out to the edges of the field from a giant birthday cake in the middle to the music of "America the Beautiful."

"Freight Train Blues"
Author unknown

I was born in Dixie in a boomer's shack,
Just a little shanty by the railroad track.
The hummin' of the drivers was my lullaby,
A freight train whistle taught me how to cry.

I've got those freight train blues, lordy, lordy, lordy,
Got 'em in the bottom of my ramblin' shoes.
Oh when the whistle blows I gotta go,
Oh lordy, guess I'm never gonna lose
Those freight train blues.

2

"Let's Start a Band!"

Columbia Records put the Colwell Brothers under contract in 1951. "Uncle" Art Satherley signed them. Satherley, a father figure to many country artists, headed Columbia's Country/Western division and was a legend in the recording industry. The brothers were then on KNBC-TV in the weekly *Tex Williams Show*, which originated at Knott's Berry Farm just east of Los Angeles, and regulars on Williams' Saturday night show on the NBC radio network. Williams was famous at the time for his recording of "Smoke, Smoke, Smoke That Cigarette," which was Capitol Records' first million-seller.

Paul, Ralph, and Steve Colwell gained a degree of notoriety in 1949 when they entered the Hillbilly Band contest at the famed Renfro Valley Barn Dance in Kentucky, and won! They were fourteen, twelve, and sixteen years old.

The brothers were making unusual waves in the world of country and western music; they hadn't come out of Nashville, they didn't speak Southern, and they weren't even country boys. But "Mountain Valley Blues," one of their singles released in 1952 and '53, was written especially for them by country Hall of Fame writer Cindy Walker, whose songs were recorded by stars from Bing Crosby to Elvis Presley to Willie Nelson. Columbia released five Colwell singles (ten songs) during that season. For the first time, other musicians joined their sessions. "A real thrill for us young guys," Steve recalled, "was having Cousin Joe Maphis, an icon in the country music field, accompany us on fiddle and guitar."

"We performed all over the place," Steve continued, "everything from a Columbia Records gala where we were part of the entertainment with country recording star Little Jimmy Dickens to a gig at the NBC studio with the NBC orchestra conducted by Robert Armbruster to supermarket openings with Tex Williams."

"I was a bit anxious when the first song the boys learned was all about rye whiskey; Ralph was only 10 years old."
—True Colwell

The Brothers were regulars on the weekly *Tex Williams Show* on NBC TV that originated at Knott's Berry Farm near Los Angeles, and on Williams' Saturday night show carried on the NBC radio network.

Knott's Berry Farm was America's first theme park, complete with a circle of covered wagons. The brothers were regular performers there. Orange groves abounded in the area, and the Pasadena Freeway, the only one in the country, ran near the Colwell home.

The Colwells performed several times with Tennessee Ernie Ford on Cliffie Stone's *Hometown Jamboree* TV show. They shared the bill at other times with Tex Ritter and Rex Allen. Their career path seemed obvious. As it happened, it wasn't.

They had been in real danger of not having a career path at all. True and Paul Colwell Sr., their parents, knew just how close a call it had been. Their son Paul had struggled with asthma since he was two years old and more times than he or his family liked to remember, it had threatened his life.

True told of an incident in 1944 when Paul was nine years old that remained vivid in her mind into her ninety-fifth year. "We found him in his room on all fours on the floor and he had turned blue. We thought we'd lost him then, but thank God that after a rush trip to emergency, he survived. After that, we found

Super Bowl practice, 1944

The Colwell's stairsteps, from Toddler Ted to just-turned-teenager Steve, 1946

a doctor who had a facility in the mountains above the Los Angeles basin. The place used to be a tuberculosis sanitarium. Paul went up there for several months that winter, and it was a 'hardy' treatment, to say the least. We went to visit him every weekend and took him things to read. He lived outdoors, slept on the ground, and went barefoot!"

"Well," Paul said later, "it was sort of like that, but not exactly. We lived in an open-air dorm. There were no windows, only screens, and, yes, we were outdoors most of the time. I built myself up in a way I had not been able to do before, especially in strengthening the muscles in my upper body that had to do with breathing. Next year I was able to do two hundred push-ups, and went on to win the school push-up and pull-up championship."

Paul considered the body building a major plus in sports (in which he was highly competitive) and with his brothers, (with whom he was also highly competitive). "I was always jealous of Ralph's cheery demeanor and easygoing ways. When we were kids, we'd get into fights and I'd pin him to the ground. Then he'd jump up with a big grin and shout, 'It's a tie!' It drove me crazy.

"In 1939, we had moved from our birthplace, Detroit, to Mattapoisett, a small whaling town on the Massachusetts coast near New Bedford. I remember snowy winters and pleasant summers and marching in the Fourth of July parade led by Grand Marshal Sid, the barber. He was the first African-American we ever knew. That's where Steve and I nearly drowned little brother Ralph while we were trying to teach him how to swim.

"We lived in a two-hundred-year-old whaling captain's house that creaked and shrieked when the storms blew in off Buzzards Bay. I was in the first grade, Steve in the third. Dad took Steve and me to a

New Bedford Whalers semipro football game on Sunday. We stopped at a café on our way home and listened on the radio as President Roosevelt announced the attack on Pearl Harbor and declared war on Japan. It was December 7, 1941.

"In the summer of '42, we moved to San Marino, California, ten miles east of Los Angeles. Dad wrote to us just before we moved, describing our new house as having a mountain 'in the backyard.' It was actually the San Gabriel Mountains, topped by Mount Wilson, that graced the horizon of the San Gabriel Valley. There was great excitement as our train rolled through the miles of orange groves under sunny blue skies and into beautiful Los Angeles Union Station.

"We played 'guns' and planted our victory garden on the nearby estate of the aunt of World War II hero General George Patton. When the war ended, we staged our own parade with our neighborhood friends marching up and down our street banging on pots and pans.

"It was an idyllic existence for kids. We were outdoors all the time, most of the year in bare feet. We would only come in at the end of the day for dinner and then sit around the radio listening to the daily half-hour episodes of *Superman, The Lone Ranger, Captain Midnight, Terry and the Pirates, Red Rider, The Cisco Kid, Hop Harrigan,* and *Jack Armstrong, the All American Boy.*

"It was nonstop sports and games: pick-up baseball on the vacant lots, football in the park, hit-the-bat in the street, kick-the-can all over the place, roller skating and Flexi-Flyer riding on the sidewalks, climbing and chin-ups on the high bars Dad constructed in our backyard, and, best of all, playing catch with Dad after supper in the front yard."

Colwell front yard, 1943, ages 6, 8, 10. Brother Ted would arrive two years later.

"It was an idyllic existence for kids. We were outdoors all the time, most of the year in bare feet. We would only come in at the end of the day for dinner and then sit around the radio listening to the daily half-hour episodes of Superman..."

Steve had a paper route. Paul mowed lawns and briefly hawked the *Los Angeles Herald Express* on a busy street corner. Ralph was supposed to mow the family lawn but would often be found lying on the uncut grass, daydreaming.

The California style was strictly blue jeans.

"All of us were bat boys for Dad's semipro baseball team," Paul said. "There were a lot of service teams that came through, and once we got Joe DiMaggio's autograph. Ted was born during a game. Dad rushed to the hospital and returned after the game ended with news of our new baby brother. That was in July 1945, one month before Hiroshima."

In late winter of 1948, something happened that would influence the future course of the brothers' lives. Steve, fourteen at the time, answered a "Special Offer" ad in *Boys' Life* and sold enough garden seeds door-to-door to earn a Gene Autry guitar. Then Paul, who was twelve, took his ten dollars in savings and bought a banjo/ukulele. One rainy Saturday afternoon, when not much was happening, Steve uttered the fateful words, "Let's start a band!"

Ralph, who had shown vocal talent from an early age, was drafted as lead vocalist, along with Chuck Buck, the boys' best friend down the street. "But I admit," True Colwell said, "I was a bit anxious when the first song they learned was all about rye whiskey. Ralph was only ten years old."

They didn't have to look far for a name for their group: The Colwell Brothers seemed to fit. Chuck Buck dropped out soon after the group was formed.

In the spring of 1948, the Armstrong Twins, the Four Star Records recording artists from Arkansas' Ozark Mountains, did some live radio shows from the KXLA studios in Pasadena's Huntington Hotel, not far from San Marino. Steve and Paul went up to watch the broadcasts and were fascinated. "It was the combination of the open ringing string sound of the mandolin and guitar and the clear blend of the twins' harmonies that hooked us," Steve explained.

"That's it," Paul remembered thinking. "A mandolin! I've got to get me one of those." It was love at first sound. Back home, they put their heads together to figure out how to duplicate what they had heard.

With Paul Sr.'s financial support, Paul bought a new mandolin. Then they started immersing themselves in country and western music, leaning a little more to the western at first. Their initial repertoire included songs by Tex Ritter,

Sons of the Pioneers, Bob Wills and the Texas Playboys, Hank Williams, and, of course, the Armstrong Twins. Then, they got hooked on the bluegrass sounds of Bill Monroe and Lester Flatt and Earl Scruggs. In a matter of a few weeks, they were developing a style they considered their own. Their first show was at a cocktail party given by their parents; Ralph sang "Rye Whiskey." His soprano voice had not yet changed. Two weeks later, they performed at an assembly program at Huntington School in San Marino.

Paul Sr.'s job took the family to Indiana in 1949. The trio entered the Indianapolis citywide amateur music competition, performed to an audience of ten thousand, and won. The next day, a three-column photo in the *Indianapolis Star* showed three cowboy-costumed singers.

Steve and Paul decided the group needed a bass. Two weeks later, Ralph was taking lessons at the Indiana Conservatory of Music and four months later, thanks again to Paul Sr., was sporting an instrument that towered well above his head. Later, when he was asked why he, the smallest, was always lugging around the biggest piece of equipment, he answered, "I chose last."

"Indianapolis was where we developed our bluegrass identity," Paul said. "We learned every Bill Monroe and the Bluegrass Boys and Flatt and Scruggs song

"Our schedule was non-stop: WLS in Chicago, WLW in Cincinnati, WHAS in Louisville, state and county fairs, fish fries, entertainment parks, and supermarket openings."

On Saturdays, they dragged themselves out of bed at 4 a.m. and Steve drove them to the small town of Anderson to play on a 6 a.m. radio show on 250-watt WCBC-FM that Paul quipped was "heard by a couple of farmers."

we could get our hands on, and tried to emulate that sound. Our very first radio appearance was on WISH, Indianapolis. It was a live broadcast quiz show called *Laugh with the Ladies*, hosted by Reed 'Chuckles' Chapman. We were doing everything from the nationally famous *Horace Heidt Show* and *Ted Mack's Original Amateur Hour* to an onstage performance with the Sammy Kaye Orchestra; 'Swing and Sway with Sammy Kaye' was the tagline. For that show, we teamed up with a young husband and wife duo and called ourselves the Wabash Ramblers. That turned out to be a brief interlude in our career, however; Dad convinced us to stick to the natural appeal we had as brothers.

"Our schedule was nonstop: WLS in Chicago, WLW in Cincinnati, WHAS in Louisville, state and county fairs, fish fries, entertainment parks. In 1949, we cut our first album as a Christmas gift for friends and family. It was titled 'Bluegrass and Sagebrush,' and was done on a now long-since extinct wire recorder. The title aptly reflects our transition during those Indiana years from western to bluegrass and country."

They ventured south into Kentucky's bluegrass country, where they entered the Hillbilly Band Contest at the famed Renfro Valley Barn Dance and won! They never got to savor their victory, however. The prize was a trip to Washington, D.C., but they couldn't go because of school, and the trophy they received listed them as "The Baldwell Brothers."

Soon the Colwells, ages seventeen, fifteen, and thirteen, were booked for a half-hour TV show in Indianapolis called *Marlene's Melodies* (named for the sponsor) that ran for several months in 1950 and into '51. On Saturdays, they dragged themselves out of bed at 4 a.m. and Steve drove them to the small town of Anderson to play on a 6 a.m. radio show on 250-watt WCBC-FM that Paul quipped was "heard by a couple of farmers." Their ride was a 1936 DeSoto. "Dad saw a For Sale sign on the windshield at an old farm house and bought it for $100," Paul said. "Top speed was 55, the steering box was loose and it weaved a lot, but it was big enough for our instruments and us."

On many weekends, they played on *Midwestern Hayride*, a major Saturday night radio show on 50,000-watt WLW in Cincinnati, hosted by country star Ernie Lee. When Paul Sr.'s business took the family back to California in the spring of 1951, they moved into a house at 1680 Sherwood Road in San Marino, which would be home base for years to come.

"In 1949 we cut our first album as a Christmas gift for friends and family. It was done on a now long since extinct wire recorder and aptly reflects our transition during those Indiana years from western to bluegrass and country."

BLUEGRASS AND SAGEBRUSH

Songs by the
COLWELL
BROTHERS

PAUL

STEVE

RALPH

CHRISTMAS
1949
"Pecos Bill"
"Bluegrass Breakdown"
"Lovesick Blues"
"Kentucky Waltz"
"Tennessee Waltz"
"Sugar Hill"

"The Further We Reach Out"

Paul Colwell, Ken Ashby, Frank Fields

I had a thought
While they walked in the moon dust,
In one breathless moment I saw,
Like warm air rising,
Or apples falling,
It must be a natural law.

> The further we reach out,
> The closer we become.
> The further we reach out,
> The closer we become.

Each time we reach out
Beyond our knowing,
Each time that we overcome,
Or breach the limits of our love,
We leave dreams for our little ones.

> The further we reach out,
> The closer we become,
> The further we reach out,
> The closer we become.

3

NUDGED INTO THE
NATIONAL SPOTLIGHT

For years, Paul Sr. had worked for one of the big three U.S. canned-food companies, rising to national sales manager. But Colwell chafed at what he felt corporate culture expected of him and in 1951, "Dad told us he had resigned his position and was taking us back to California," Ralph said. "The company had offered him a big promotion and pay increase to stay, but he'd turned them down. There was something in his character that told him to leave the hard-drinking, hard-driving corporate culture of the day and strike out on his own. I think that was a deeply moral decision, and Dad risked everything to preserve his own sense of decency and family values. We didn't realize it then, but his decision changed all of our lives. It was a hinge point."

In California, Paul Sr. not only found success in business, he also found an agent for his talented sons. Cliff Carling, it turned out, was also the agent for Tex Williams, which led to the brothers becoming regulars on Williams' radio and TV shows. In combination with the recordings they were making for Columbia Records, exposure on the Williams shows nudged the Colwells into the national spotlight.

Then in early July, a friend arranged tickets for them to see the Hollywood premiere of *Jotham Valley*, a musical running at the Carthay Circle Theater. Ironically, the show was about rancher brothers who were feuding over water rights. Ralph remembered enjoying the performance, but most of all meeting cast members after the show.

"Mountain Valley Blues" was written for the Colwell Brothers by Country Hall of Fame legend Cindy Walker. Columbia Records released five Colwell singles (ten songs) in 1952-'53.

Accepting an invitation to a musical show had unforeseen consequences for the three brothers. "A lot of the cast were young," Steve recalled, "and they had some exciting ideas. We were intrigued with their sense of purpose."

"A lot of them were young," Steve recalled, "and easy to talk with. They had some exciting ideas. We were intrigued by their sense of purpose."

Jotham Valley was presented by Moral Re-Armament (MRA), a nonprofit international organization working to bring about positive social changes. "We liked the people," Steve said, "and thought about what we'd heard."

A few days later, they took their parents to see the show. After the final curtain, they went backstage to talk with the cast again, and a lasting connection began.

On July 16, the family visited the organization's Los Angeles headquarters. "There was a party going on," Paul recalled. "It was the birthday of a Scottish guy named Eric Millar. He was at a grand piano playing a mix of boogie and jazz for everybody and I thought, 'Hey, this could be fun.' The man could play."

That afternoon Frank Buchman, Moral Re-Armament's founder, showed up at the party while the Colwells were gathered around Millar at the piano. "Dr. Buchman took one look at what was going on," True said later, "and went back to his room to change his business jacket for a sport coat and a colorful tie."

Before long, the Colwells invited cast members to their home to visit, and offered to host a few of them. Soon, they were volunteering some of their time to help promote the program.

"I can remember vividly when I was a college student stuffing envelopes for a mail-out at the Los Angeles center," Steve said. "I thought to myself, 'Wow, I'm playing a part in changing the world.' Something in me responded to helping in a program that was bigger than my small world and life as an average, albeit busy, college student.

"This feeling, this new energy soon found legs in our music. We began to think about ways of expressing in song what we were experiencing. Our repertoire to that point had consisted mostly of popular country songs. Paul had written our first original song, called 'Hillbilly Heart.' But now we began looking for different content with a more positive spin and decided to try writing some new material together. That effort produced 'Come On Folks' and 'Spankin' New Day.' Paul commented later that these may have been naïve and idealistic, and 'certainly not great writing,' but Columbia Records deemed them acceptable enough to record. We had set off on a new tack."

The senior Colwells embraced the "new tack" alongside their sons. Paul Sr.'s social conscience in his business dealings would provide a concrete example for the brothers to talk about in faraway countries. True Colwell stepped outside her suburban comfort zone and developed friendships with people she normally would not have met, from Hollywood film lots to L.A.'s inner city. During a visit to San Francisco where the brothers performed for a gathering of educators and politicians from the state capital, she addressed the crowd, telling of the new direction her family had taken. With a friend, she called several times on the mother of actor Anthony Quinn, who told fascinating stories of her youth in Mexico and of Quinn's Irish-Mexican father who rode with Pancho Villa in revolutionary days. True had no way of knowing then of a family connection in the future.

Scottish jazz pianist Eric Millar intrigued the brothers during a visit to Moral Re-Armament's Los Angeles headquarters.

At the end of the school year, the brothers were invited to visit Michigan's Mackinac Island, where for more than a decade MRA had operated a conference center. The conferences, they learned, were globally oriented, focusing on

Historic Mackinac Island   *Photo by: John Penrod*

A cross-country road trip took the brothers to an international conference at Michigan's Mackinac Island, home of the Grand Hotel, which boasts of having "The Longest Porch in the World."

reconstruction of postwar Europe and Japan, conflict resolution within and between nations, and nation building in the newly independent countries of Africa.

Oliver Saul, a veteran teacher who lived near the Colwells' home, was planning to attend and agreed to accompany the boys and a friend. They traveled in two cars, one of them stuffed to the roof with Ralph's acoustic bass. They drove around the clock, stopping only once to sleep under a tree in a park at Gaylord, Michigan, just a couple of hours away from the island.

In his younger years, Saul had been a cowboy in Wyoming, and was a member of the posse that captured the last train bandit in America. Tough, smart, and organized, he was famed for his rope tricks and was quite used to lassoing teenagers. Saul's youngest son, Don, who had also been a cowboy in his youth, remembered hearing about the trip to Michigan.

"Pop arrived at the Colwells' home to pick up the guys and found them playing basketball instead of packing their stuff. He took a very dim view of that." "Pop" Saul would later become Ralph's tutor as he completed his high school studies on the road.

At Mackinaw City, on the northern tip of Michigan's lower peninsula, the travelers boarded Arnold Transit Co.'s *Islander*, a hard-working eighty-foot coal-fired ferry, and joined other passengers and tons of freight for the forty-five-minute trip across the Straits of Mackinac.

The ferry trip was spectacular. A giant Great Lakes ore boat pushed a massive bow wave as it churned southbound through the straits, loaded to the gunnels with ore from Minnesota's Iron Range destined for some blast furnace in a steel mill in Illinois. Pleasure yachts dotted the lake, their sails filled by a springtime breeze, glowing in the sun. Paul remembered thinking it looked like a postcard.

"On the left side of the boat as we got closer to the island," Ralph recalled, "we could see the Grand Hotel, which was famous for having the longest porch in the world—660 feet."

As the *Islander* snuggled in alongside the dock, its passengers seemed to enter another era. There were no motorized vehicles in sight; in fact, the only one on the island was a forties fire truck, judiciously not on display. Main Street, the town's one and only thoroughfare, greeted them with a line of carriages. The backbench of the carriage that took them on the ten-minute trot to the conference center was dedicated to Ralph's bass. Gracious summer homes along the way were interspersed with multistoried fifty-year-old guesthouses.

"I remember that a grand mix of three fragrances assailed our nostrils that day," Steve said, "manure, fudge, and lilacs. You couldn't miss the horses. Then there was that famous Mackinac fudge. And lilacs were in bloom all along the road and around the schoolhouse. We were pretty tired, but it was exciting to be experiencing it all."

The whirlwind of conference activities that began the next day catapulted the Colwells from lives of classes, careers, and country music into an environment focused on making a difference in society. "That focus resonated with the values we'd been exposed to at home," Paul said.

It also resonated with their passion for music. Conference addresses were interspersed with songs from a colorfully costumed international chorus. Now the meetings were enlivened by the addition of the trio of Hollywood cowboys who introduced a disarming new element for visitors from overseas. Their costumes added to the impression.

"They came from Nudie's," Paul said. "Nudie's Rodeo Tailors was the premier outfitter for all the big country and western stars. I remember going up to his place on Victory Boulevard in North Hollywood and playing mandolin for Nudie and Bobby, his wife. Nudie also played mandolin and loved to jam."

Mackinac was the scene of the first engagement between British and American forces in the War

The backbench of the carriage that took them on the ten-minute trot to the conference center was dedicated to Ralph's bass.

of 1812, and an important site for the Chippewa and Ottawa tribes of the region. The Native Americans had named it "mish-la-mack-in-aw," or "big turtle," as its outline was seen to resemble a gigantic hard-shelled reptile. They had considered the island a neutral site where warring tribes could powwow to find solutions to their conflicts. Scores of Native American families lived in a group of homes in the center of the island, known then as Indian Village. Children from the Village attended the Island School on Main Street, where that fall Phyllis Kaempfer was to begin her first year as a teacher.

She invited the Colwells to sing at the Village just before classes were to start. "Scotty MacFarland, an effervescent character who worked with MRA, hired a flatbed wagon and loaded the Colwells and me onto it," remembered Kaempfer. "As we drove along the hard-packed old road that ran through the Village, we kept stopping for the Colwells to sing and play from the wagon bed and for Scotty to exclaim to the folks in a very loud voice, 'You'll really look after this teacher and be kind to her, won't you?'"

Theatrical productions took place in the evenings. "Some of the popular numbers we sang before the shows and in the meetings were bluegrass and country songs like 'Black Strap Molasses' and 'Morgan Poisoned the Water Hole,'" Paul said. "We were busy all the time but we had a lot of fun that summer."

It would be more than a decade before the Colwells would return to Mackinac, in circumstances they could not possibly have imagined.

Back in California in the fall, they set an astounding pace for themselves: In addition to recording for Columbia and appearing live on the *Tex Williams Show* every week, they kept on top of their schoolwork and performed and spoke at local MRA events. Steve played varsity baseball for Occidental College and was vice president of his sophomore class; Paul played basketball for South Pasadena High and was on the student council; Ralph was an aggressive running back on the school's "B" football team averaging ten yards per carry and was vice president of his sophomore class.

They finished their classes the following spring, unaware that in forty-five days they would be singing on another continent, in another language, for a founding father of the embryonic European Union.

The Colwells at their
Sherwood Road home in
San Marino in 1953, just
before the brothers' world
tours would begin. Ted
was eight years old.

"Tre Ragazzi"
Angelo Pasetto

Eravamo tre ragazzi,
Senza molto volontà.
Sempre allegro, molto pazzi,
Forse più de la metà."

(We're three ordinary guys,
Carefree as can be.
Always happy, pretty crazy,
Maybe more than you can see.)

4

HAVE XYLOPHONE,
WILL TRAVEL

Herb Allen showed up at Mackinac Island in 1946, six years before the Colwells. He was sixteen, eager to make the trip, and found it no hardship to sit up in a railway coach for ninety-six hours from Seattle to Detroit. Allen marveled at the panorama speeding along outside his window. From Detroit, he hitchhiked north to the Straits of Mackinac.

During the final two hours on the highway, "a cynical know-it-all who'd given me a ride bombarded me with about a hundred reasons why I should immediately turn around and go home," he remembered. The diatribe startled the young traveler, but failed to stop him; he'd faced opposition about this venture even before he left home.

Allen had just completed his junior year at Seattle's Lincoln High School. At the start of that year, he had gone with his parents to see *The Forgotten Factor*, a touring stage drama about two families, one labor and one management. It was a play about teamwork in industry, but it was the people who stirred his imagination.

"They had a kind of infectious quality," Herb recalled. "I was intrigued and went backstage to meet them. They'd just come from Mackinac Island, and it was the first time I'd heard about MRA and what was happening there. I would describe what I saw that evening as adventure connected with a purpose. I wanted to be part of it."

At Mackinac, Allen was not disappointed. He met visitors from many countries. "It was both inspiring and

A classically trained virtuoso from Seattle dazzled an international audience in June 1947. 18-year old Herb Allen's first xylophone performance at the Michigan conference drew bravos in a number of languages.

Now Being Circulated

He Knows His Rhythm!

**Whittier Preschool
Association Feb. 8**

The Whittier Preschool Association will hold its regular monthly meeting on Wednesday, Feb. 8th, at 2 p. m., in the school auditorium.

Ethel-Ann Reinig, organizer of the Seattle Baby Orchestra, will speak on "Developing Music in the Preschool Child." She will present several of her soloists (preschool age).

THEY CAN'T BEAT MY TIME

HERBIE ALLEN, three, is the world's youngest drummer, according to Ethel-Ann Reinig, director of the Seattle Baby Orchestra in which he plays.—(Post-Intelligencer Photo.)

The youngest drummer in the world!

That's the claim Ethel-Ann Reinig, director of the Seattle Baby Orchestra, makes for Herbie Allen, three, son of Mr. and Mrs. Herbert Allen, 8541 Burke Ave.

Herbie plays the snare, bass drum, triangle and tambourine with the skill of a professional and a perfect sense of rhythm, according to Miss Reinig.

The baby orchestra, of which Herbie is the drummer, has sixteen members. The oldest is seven years. They will play for the preschool entertainments at Daniel Bagley and Green Lake schools today.

Miss Ethel-Ann Reinig

Herb Allen's teacher declared him "The World's Youngest Drummer" when he was three. "He plays the snare, bass drum, triangle and tambourine with the skill of a professional and a perfect sense of rhythm."

realistic. 'If you want to change the world,' they were saying, 'start with yourself.' I could think of plenty of places to do that! And for me as a musician, it was great to see how they utilized music and theater as a sort of 'show window' for the endeavor."

At summer's end, Herb wanted to stay on and travel with the troupe, but his parents insisted he return to Seattle and graduate from high school. "See you next year," he promised a friend as he boarded the *Islander* to start the trip back home.

Allen was a serious musician, already renowned as a xylophone virtuoso. The list of his music and stage credentials had been building since he was a toddler. He may have been predestined to be a percussionist. His mother, Dot (she was christened Lilian, but known as Dot since childhood because she was tiny), recalled that when she was sixteen, she often heard xylophone music coming from a certain house as she walked home after classes. "If I ever have a son," she'd mused, "that's what he'll play."

"Did she put some mallets in my hand the moment I was born?" Herb once asked. "You know, I'm really not sure! But definitely within the first couple of weeks, I learned later."

Ethel-Ann Reinig, director of the Seattle Baby Orchestra, first presented her protégé, "Herbie," in solo performance when he was three years old, touting him as "The Youngest Drummer in the World."

"He plays the snare, bass drum, triangle and tambourine with the

WEDNESDAY, OCTOBER 17, 1934.

skill of a professional and a perfect sense of rhythm," she declared to the *Seattle Post-Intelligencer* and other local newspapers. Baby Orchestra members were all age seven or under except for the pianist, who was twelve.

Herb performed frequently in vaudeville. During World War II, he played in a U.S. Savings Bond benefit that featured Al Jolson. He studied under Seattle's leading teachers, Carl Pitzer and then John Hopper, to become a concert pianist. At fifteen, he started a dance band, Herbie Allen and His Orchestra. It was hardly what his parents expected after his intensive classical training. Their son had been working diligently, they knew, so diligently that they worried about the circles under his eyes when he came down to breakfast. What they didn't know was that after dinner when he went to his

At four, Allen was conducting the Seattle Baby Orchestra. All the members were age seven or under, except for the pianist, who was twelve.

room and closed his door to study, he would often climb out his window and set off for some gig with his band.

"I had been studying classical music for years, but when Mom realized I was serious about branching out, she bought me Hazel Scott's Boogie Woogie Exercises. Well, 'if you can't beat 'em, join 'em.' We still played duets at home, though."

From ages five to sixteen, Herb performed on KJR Radio's Uncle Frank's Children's Hour, for which he learned and presented a new song every week. An early lesson in diplomacy came one Saturday morning when he was twelve. While he was playing baseball with friends on Burke Avenue in front of his house, Herb hit a fly ball "that went where it wasn't supposed to; it wasn't supposed to go through the living room window!" That afternoon on Uncle Frank's Children's Hour, Herb dedicated his piece to his father, who he knew would be listening on his way home from work.

In June 1943 the president of the Seattle Chamber of Commerce wrote Allen a letter: "Dear Herbert: I was much interested when I read in a newspaper the other day that you had offered your German Shepherd, Smarty, to the Coast Guard for combat duty. I realize what a sacrifice this means to a boy, and I think you have demonstrated commendable patriotism in your willingness to give up your pal. I, too, hope that Smarty will be assigned to the Red Cross, 'so she won't have to hurt anybody.' Yours very truly, D.K. MacDonald, President."

Hearing that his young protégé planned to return to Mackinac in 1947, John Hopper was "beyond belief unhappy," Herb recalled. "I was already enrolled at Oberlin School of Music in Ohio and looking ahead to Juilliard. Mr. Hopper spent a whole lesson (that I'd paid for) trying to talk me out of it! 'You're throwing away a career,' he insisted. It was a difficult hour. I didn't take lightly what he'd said. After all, he was probably the leading teacher in the Northwest. I knew he had my best interests at heart. But something was compelling me to be part of what I had experienced at the island. Mom and Dad and I talked it over at great length." The next summer, with his parents' blessing, Herb returned to Michigan.

In 1947, fresh out of high school, Allen became part of a theatrical team that included prolific Scottish composer George Fraser and London's Dr. William Reed. Reed immediately took Allen under his wing as assistant music director of MRA's

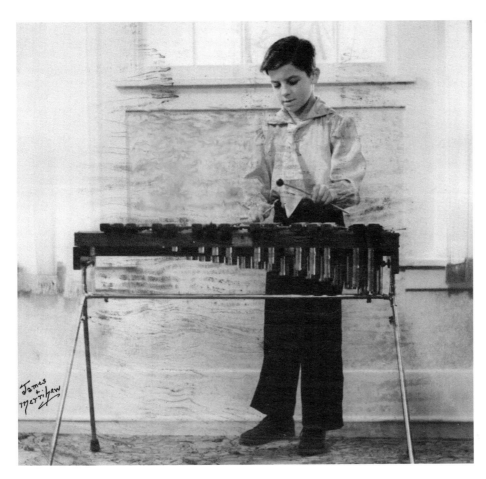

The maestro at ten.

new musical revue, *The Good Road*, which would be shown that winter in New York, Boston, Montreal, Ottawa, and in Washington, D.C. to a third of America's senators and representatives.

Asked later what an assistant music director did, Herb quipped, "Well, I was setting up music stands and playing triangle in the orchestra. Of course, in reality, I put myself at the feet of Will Reed to learn everything he would teach me. He was a master." When Reed died in 2002, the *London Times* devoted a full page to his obituary.

In the spring of 1948, Allen set sail for Europe aboard the Cunard Line's aging SS *Aquitania*, headed to participate in a global conference at a storybook hotel at Caux-sur-Montreux in Switzerland. The property, once a fashionable resort, was used as a sanctuary for refugees during World War II.

SEATTLE CHAMBER OF COMMERCE

OFFICE OF THE PRESIDENT

215 COLUMBIA STREET
MAIN 5060
SEATTLE, WASHINGTON (4)
June 25, 1943

Allen offered his German Shepherd, Smarty, to the Coast Guard for combat duty. The president of the Seattle Chamber of Commerce read about it in a newspaper. "I realize what a sacrifice this means to a boy," he wrote in a letter, "and I think you have demonstrated commendable patriotism in your willingness to give up your pal. I, too, hope that Smarty will be assigned to the Red Cross, 'so she won't have to hurt anybody.'"

Swiss citizens, several of whom had visited MRA's Mackinac center immediately after the war, had acquired the property as a center for European reconciliation. The first meetings of French and Germans after World War II took place there on the mountainside.

By the time Allen and company arrived at Caux, ripples of what was happening there were being felt across the continent. Dr. Konrad Adenauer, then president of the Parliamentary Council of the three Western-occupied zones of Germany, visited Caux in 1948 and urged that The Good Road and The Forgotten Factor be brought to his country. Invitations arrived from West German state cabinets, and the British, American, and French occupation authorities pledged to support the visit with all the facilities they could make available.

New stage sets were constructed, and Herb and the music specialists began teaching *The Good Road* cast a German version of the play's theme song, "Der Gute Weg." The show itself, however, would be presented in English. It was Allen's first exposure to the multiple-language environments he would live and work in for decades to come.

Quite apart from being the first multinational civilian group to enter Germany following the war, *The Good Road* tour broke new technical ground. Into Allen's hands were put not a xylophone or piano, but several 33 1/3 rpm phonograph discs and a record player with a three-quarter inch needle.

When the move into Germany was confirmed, Will Reed flew to Los Angeles. With the backing of such luminaries as director Mervyn LeRoy; actors Joel McCrea and Reginald Owen; and John Trancatella, president of the local musicians union, an orchestra of leading symphony and studio artists was brought together to put the instrumental track of *The Good Road* on newly developed long-playing vinyl records. A historic agreement by the musicians and their union leaders allowed the recordings to become the "orchestra" for the show. It would be Herb Allen's job, from beginning to end of the two-hour production, to drop the needle of the record player in exactly the right groove at the exact moment a specific number was to begin. "By the time we'd completed the rehearsals," Herb said, "I could recite every cue in my sleep."

Twenty-eight days after the invitation from Adenauer, at 7:30 a.m. on October 9, 1948, a cavalcade of brightly painted Swiss buses rolled out of Zurich, headed for Munich. Herb sat behind the driver of the third bus. On board were 260 people from a dozen countries. Some had fought against Germany; some had survived Nazi occupation. Irène Laure, who had led the socialist women of France, was among them. Her son had been tortured by the Gestapo, yet she had found the courage to relinquish her hatred of the Germans.

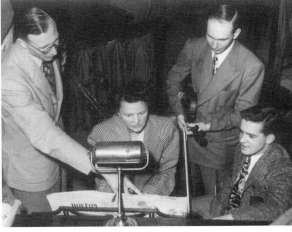

Dr. Will Reed, here with pianist Frances Hadden and violinist Melville Carson, made Allen assistant music director of the new musical review, *The Good Road*. Allen was 18.

The company set sail for Europe in June 1948 on the SS *Aquitania*. It was the last crossing for the venerable Cunard liner, the first of many for Allen.

MRA's conference center at Caux sur Montreux, Switzerland was the site of the first meetings between the Germans and the French after World War II.

CAUX

Two days later, in the war-damaged Munich Opera House, the curtain opened on *The Good Road*. Thousands came, and hundreds remained to talk; their visitors were the first foreigners other than soldiers that they had seen since the war. In Munich, as in Stuttgart, Frankfurt, Düsseldorf, and Essen, multiple performances were needed because of the crowds. Invariably, a few puzzled people would look into the orchestra pit for the musicians.

Herb and his friend Bill Baumann got to know Hans Jorg Gareis, a Prussian general's son who would later work with them in volatile areas of the Middle East and Europe. In 1953, former Marshall Plan administration chief Paul Hoffman would refer to Moral Re-Armament's initiatives as "the ideological counterpart of the Marshall Plan."

The Good Road moved on from Germany for performances in The Hague, then to London for an engagement at His Majesty's Theatre. The winter of 1948 was cold and damp. Herb remembered fog so thick "that to walk across the street carried with it the peril of a taxi passing by inches away, driven by an intrepid cabbie who somehow always knew where he was, even if pedestrians like me could hardly see our hand stretched out in front of us."

Additions to the company began arriving by air from the United States, and Herb, along with Dr. Reed and George Fraser, worked to train and integrate the new cast members. The show would open on November 10. Early that morning, Herb wrote a letter to his folks:

"Setting: a room with two beds, a handy sink basin, closet, dressers, a gas stove/fireplace with meter and coin slot for heat (the coin box is left open intentionally for the inhabitants' continual use of the same shilling), a teakettle on a little gas stove, two boys sitting before the fire writing to their families—Rolf Ulfrstad of Norway and Herbie Allen his roommate. Today is the premiere of *The Good Road* in London and Rolf, a violinist, and Herbie, a xylophonist, eagerly look forward to the evening."

Ten days into *The Good Road*'s sold-out London engagement (the show now had a live orchestra) Herb and Baumann were asked to return to Germany to work in the Ruhr, the heart of Germany's vital coal industry and an essential component of European recovery. A German-language version of *The Forgotten Factor* would open in late November in a hall near the ruins of the giant Krupp works in Essen. The audience was packed with workers, managers, and a number of cabinet ministers.

Some of the spectators were colorfully costumed during an impromptu concert on the Caux lawn.

The cold war was escalating rapidly, and control of coal production in the Ruhr was a major objective of the Soviet Union. For Herb and Bill, that winter was a crash course in dealing with conflict. Their mentors were two canny, good-natured Scottish army veterans who had served in the Italian campaign during the war. Both were skilled in building industrial teamwork. Soon the young Americans were interacting with miners, managers, company directors, and their families.

"I learned the importance of language quickly," Herb recalled. "I was needing a haircut, and as I'd been picking up a little German, I strolled into a barber shop one day and said to the man, 'Ein bischen Kurtz, bitte.' Well, I didn't know it but apparently I'd asked for a coal miner's cut. I walked out of there with the first American Mohawk!"

The following May, six months after they'd arrived in Germany, Allen and Baumann returned to Caux, along with a cadre of miners and industrialists. A film version of *The Good Road* was being shot in Lausanne, halfway to Geneva

Germany in 1948: hope amidst the rubble.

along the north shore of the lake, and they commuted frequently to help with the production. Off the set, if there were lulls in the shooting and Herb had access to a piano, admirers would surround him.

One morning as the summer's activities were winding down, Herb and Bill, their Scottish teammates, and a handful of others were asked to gather in a small meeting room. There, a group of Italians, representing fifty of their compatriots including the visionary Countess Cicogna, invited Allen and his friends to shift their focus to Italy. The countess during the sessions of the conference had recognized the disarming quality of the young Americans. Open hearts, she reasoned, could open doors in her country. The invitation was accepted.

"First we needed to learn Italian," Herb said. "We spent four months at the Berlitz language school in Lugano. By the time we left there, we were thinking in Italian, dreaming even. Then we began meeting people in the industrial towns near Milan, where we'd arrived with just enough money to last for three days.

"I got to know Bruno Golumberti. He was an active communist who lived in Sesto San Giovanni, where the big Falk steelworks were located. Sesto was known all over Italy as 'Little Stalingrad.' After the war, there'd been ugly riots there. Two factory managers were thrown alive into the blast furnaces and over a hundred people were shot down in the streets. It supposedly happened because of the communist/fascist struggles, but some of it was to pay off old grudges. Bruno had grown up in the middle of all this. He was about twenty-four then, a few years older than me. Before long, he invited me to come stay with his family. They were wonderful people, wholehearted in everything they expressed and everything they did. When Bruno was with his friends, the language was colorful, to say the least. I learned a lot of Italian there that for some reason they hadn't taught me at Berlitz.

"One evening, I looked under my bed and found a machine gun. Well, I'd grown up in Seattle, Washington, USA, I was still only nineteen, and, you know, I wasn't really used to that sort of thing.

"'Hey, what's worrying you?' Bruno asked me, when I 'happened' to mention my 'discovery.' 'We all have machine guns here. There's one in every apartment in the block.'

"'OK, Herb,' I thought, 'we're not in Kansas anymore!'"

There were a dozen other international volunteers working with Allen and

Overflow crowds in German cities meant that extra performances of *The Good Road* had to be given.

In Italy (left) Herb composed all the time. "Melodies flowed out of him like water."

Baumann in and around the Milan area. "We really needed an operations base," Herb recalled. "Then, through the kindness of Principessa Castelbarco, we were offered temporary use of a palazzo that had been vacant for fifteen years. The building was scheduled to be demolished in six months, but it was a perfect setting for what we wanted to accomplish during that time. The

Between takes during filming of *The Good Road* in Lausanne, Switzerland in 1949, Allen drew a crowd.

only problem was that we didn't have any resources to make it operable except muscles and sweat."

For two weeks, they cleaned and painted. "Then, to our amazement, money and other contributions began coming in. Workers we visited in the evenings gave us beds and other furniture, and employees from Montecatini Industries sent up a piano from their recreation center."

Herb was telling this story to a journalist sometime later, and at that point went quiet. After a few moments, he slowly shook his head. "Think about that," he said. "Italian workers in the 1950s weren't in the habit of loading up visiting Americans with gifts. Yes, they appreciated American aid. But they didn't like Americans. What connected us with Bruno and others was that we were just ourselves. They knew we were dedicated to the concept that if people changed the way they thought and lived they could change society, and as communists they could relate to that. In one sense that commitment 'out radicalized' their revolution, because it challenged people equally on both sides of the barricade.

"We became friends during those days with Angelo Pasetto, a fine playwright and poet who previously had written marching songs for the Communist Party. I had put together a chorus. Some members were workers, some were students, and some were factory managers and directors. We focused on music themed around unity and a positive future. Pasetto was really quite captured by this concept, and saw a new focus for his talents. He wrote some wonderful songs for us that we sang all over the country. There was one that Bill and I sang with Jerry Von Teuber, who worked with us for a long time in Italy. The audience especially loved that song, and it was a while before we realized just how much we three Americans were poking fun at ourselves in it."

During that time, Herb composed music daily. Bill's sister, Lorraine Baumann, an accomplished musician, was also volunteering in Italy. She marveled at Allen's talent. "Melodies flowed out of him like water," she said.

Bruno was the leader of the Alpine Club, an intrepid group of mountain climbers, Herb recalled. "They'd go up into the mountains each weekend to escape the dull, gray atmosphere of Sesto. One day, they took Bill and me along. On the way up, they showed us the crosses of friends they had lost climbing there, the last one only two months before. He had fallen eight hundred feet. After this encouraging sight, they proceeded to tie ropes around Bill and me. Up we went. I was scared stiff. When it came time to rappel down, I grabbed hold of the mountain and shouted 'Mama mia!' From then on, the Alpine Club dubbed it the Mama Mia Mountain."

Allen and Californian Bill Baumann worked for years in Italy, where their attitude and music opened hearts and doors.

Herb and his friends were frequently in the home of the director of one of the 250 factories of Montecatini, Italy's giant chemical combine. "The workers hated Fortunato Monguzzi," Herb said. But Monguzzi loved Herb's music, and never missed an opportunity to have the young musician trundle his xylophone into his house to entertain guests. "Monguzzi spent many hours talking with us during those months. Eventually, he went to his union leader, who'd been a party member for forty years, and apologized for his aloof and arrogant attitude. This opened up a level of trust and cooperation that hadn't existed before. Strikes in Italy's chemical industry dropped the next year from fifty to five."

In 1952, ten months before he would link up with the Colwell brothers and just before his twenty-third birthday, Herb and some friends were in

Assisi, the home of St. Francis, and a site of veneration for millions across the world. After a thoughtful visit to the Basilica of San Francesco, Herb found a small trattoria where a piano was tucked away behind the few tables of the cafe. There, in a little less than two hours, he composed a musical setting for St. Francis' immortal prayer. The work has been performed on every continent, and often been called a classic.

"La Preghiera di San Francesco"

Oh! Signore, fa' di me
Un istrumento della tua pace:
Dove è odio, fa' ch'io porti l'Amore,
Dov'è offesa, ch'io porti'l Perdono,
Dovè discordia, ch'io porti l'Unione,
Dove è dubbio, ch'io porti la Fede,
Dov'è errore, ch'io porti la Verità,
Dov'è disperazione, ch'io porti la Speranza,
Dove'è tristezza, ch'io porti la Gioia,
Dove sono le tenebre, ch'io porti la Luce.
Oh! Maestro, fa' che io non cerchi tanto
Ad esser consolato, quanto a consolare,
Ad esser compreso, quanto a comprendere,
Ad esser amato, quanto ad amare.
Poichè si è dando, che si è riceve,
Perdonando che si è perdonati,
Morendo, che si risucita
A Vita Eterna.

Lord, I pray thee, make of me
An instrument Thy perfect peace to bring
Where there is hatred may I bring love,
Where there is malice may I bring pardon,
Where there is discord may I bring harmony,
Where there is doubt may I bring faith,
Where there is error may I bring truth,
Where there is despair may I bring hope,
Where there is sadness may I bring joy,
Where there is darkness may I bring light.
Oh! Master, may I seek
Not so much to be comforted as to comfort,
To be understood as to show understanding,
To be loved as to love.
For it is in giving that we receive,
In forgiving that we shall be forgiv'n,
In dying that we shall rise up
To life eternal.
  —Translated by Marshall Cartledge

"We Are Many, We Are One"

Paul and Ralph Colwell, Herb Allen

We live on the Amazon, live on the Nile,
The tropic shore and Pacific isle.
We built the Parthenon and Chinese wall,
Seen armies conquer and empires fall.
We fought for our dignity, fought for our place,
There's a different story in every face,
The book isn't written, it's only begun,
It's starting to dawn like the morning sun.

We are many, we are one,
Brothers and sisters,
Wherever you're from.
We all dance to a different drum,
We are many but we are one.

5

SIGNING ON TO REMAKE THE WORLD

By the close of 1955, the Colwell Brothers had experienced an extraordinary journey. In 1953, they flew with their parents to Switzerland, arriving at Moral Re-Armament's Caux conference center just in time to perform for Swiss National Day. They quickly became favorites of the international delegates, who had never heard or seen anything quite like the young Americans. In addition to their country and bluegrass songs, they wrote and sang new material reflecting the themes and aims of the conference, special songs for delegates from different countries, and numbers poking fun at the foibles of human nature.

"They even had the audacity to yodel to the Swiss," said their father, who after a month returned home with True to run his business. Theo Spoerri, rector of the University of Zurich, wrote to a friend: "I have lived all my life in Switzerland, but I have never heard a Swiss who can out-yodel these Colwell brothers."

One of the most delighted with the Colwell's arrival was Herb Allen. Swiss National Day, August 1st, 1953, was day one of a lifelong collaboration. The brothers performed with Allen several times that summer.

Three weeks into the conference, dressed in their custom-made outfits from Nudie's Rodeo Tailors—cowboy hats, boots, western shirts and pants, and string ties—they sang in French to Robert Schuman, the former French foreign minister. Ralph said Swiss friends helped them write the song, and it was their first non-English performance.

The Colwell Brothers arrived in Caux on Swiss National Day and were an immediate hit. They even had the audacity to yodel to the Swiss!

Three weeks into the conference the brothers sang in French to Robert Schuman, the former foreign minister of France. It was their first non-English performance. They would eventually sing in thirty-seven languages and dialects.

"We wrote it the day before Schuman came, learned it the day he was here, and sang it on his departure the next morning. At least, I thought we had learned it," Ralph said. "He came out the front door with Dr. Buchman and we were waiting there, with the international chorus all in costume just behind us. Paul played an intro, Steve sang the first verse, and damned if I could remember that stupid French chorus! I got a little less than half of the words right. Everyone was in hysterics, even Frank and Schuman. Paul said it was hard for him to sing the words right 'due to adverse conditions.' I have my suspicions they were laughing at us and not with us, but Schuman obviously loved it."

~

Late in August, they went boating on Lake Geneva with three of their new friends, including Don Saul, a U.S. Navy veteran; Eric Millar, the talented Scottish musician and navy veteran they had met in California; and Vere James from England, who had served in the Royal Navy. Evidently, it took three experienced sailors to assure the boys' safety in what was basically a good-sized rowboat.

"Of course," said Ralph, "Vere James had discreetly informed us he was the youngest officer in the British Navy to run a ship aground! It was a gorgeous Swiss summer day and we were floating just off historic Chateau de Chillon soaking in the sunshine. Then our friends dropped the bombshell that Dr. Buchman had invited us to spend the next year traveling and performing as part of MRA's full-time staff. I nearly fell out of the boat. We had been so impressed with the people we'd been working with and the cause they were dedicating their lives to that the invitation nearly took my breath away. We had come to Europe that summer to spend just one month, which we'd already extended. We had to get back to L.A. to continue school and our music career.

"The invitation presented us with a serious dilemma. There was no question that we would love to do it if we could, but could we? Steve was in the middle of his undergraduate work at Occidental College in Los Angeles, Paul was entering college, and I had two more years of high school to complete."

The brothers talked with their family in California by phone, and telegrams and letters went flying back and forth across the Atlantic.

Paul wrote that the invitation "… caught us by surprise. We had plane reservations to fly home on September 18th. Dr. Buchman specifically made clear that having us with him would depend on whether 'it was in complete accord with the family's plans and wishes.'"

"On one hand we were very taken with the program," Steve recalled, "and were committed to pursue our newfound goals. On the other, we knew we'd be kissing our recording and TV careers, as well as our college educations, goodbye at least for a year. For me it was a gut-wrenching decision. Ralph would be sacrificing his last two years of high school and playing on the football team. Dad especially questioned the wisdom of this, and wanted to make sure we understood all we were giving up. Dad had always supported our music, and wouldn't now be able to attend any more of our shows. Years later, our mother told us how hard this decision had been for him. He'd actually been in tears, she said. And for all the ensuing years we would be working with MRA, they were both totally involved in it with us. Ted, who was eight when he learned we weren't coming home, said, 'They're rats and cheaters.'"

The Colwells met Herb Allen on Swiss National Day in 1953, and they performed together that summer for sessions of the conferences at Caux. Their collaboration would last a lifetime.

Japanese Prime Minister Nobusuke Kishi arriving at Caux in 1961 was given a colorful welcome from the Colwell Brothers, a costumed international chorus, and conference delegates from dozens of countries.

In a letter home, Paul outlined the brothers' decision-making process:

"Many things enter into our decision—fears, obligations, etc. The points we've been going over have probably occurred to you: 1) Ralph's schooling, football, friends. 2) Interrupting our college education; Ralph would certainly have to be tutored. 3) Our relationship with Occidental. 4) Our contracts in the show business and with Columbia Records. 5) Clothes, medicine, music and musical equipment. 6) Teddy—especially Ted; his brothers tooting off and leaving him. I figured we would write him a card every other day or so. 7) Both of you, of course, having three of your sons away from home. We're aware of the cost. We would write all those to whom we're obligated, to let them know what's happening and why, and that this isn't a vacation trip around the world."

This was a second hinge point in the Colwell Brothers' lives. "It would be hard to understand all that happened next," Ralph said later, "without knowing something about Moral Re-Armament. Our story is not about MRA, but without it our experiences would never have happened.

"When we'd returned to California from Indianapolis in 1951, my brothers and I were glad to be back in the land of surf and sun. We looked forward to continuing our music career, but just as much to school and the beach and seeing friends from earlier years. It was perhaps the twilight of Southern

California's golden age. Then we were invited to see *Jotham Valley*. We'd never heard of Moral Re-Armament, this group with the strange name, but our friends assured us that we'd love the show. And we did. It was Broadway quality: great music; a gripping story; and a large, engaging cast. We were fascinated to learn they came from many countries.

In 1954 and '55 the Colwells performed in Denmark, Italy, Germany, Switzerland, England, and Ireland.

"Before long, we learned what Moral Re-Armament was all about. At the time, MRA owned a striking old multistoried building on Flower Street in downtown Los Angeles. They called it The Club because it had been the Women's Athletic Club in years gone by. That's where we first met Dr. Buchman. He was a charismatic seventy-one-year-old who had been partially crippled by a stroke, but who was able to charm us California teenagers with his wit and a certain joie de vivre. MRA's purpose, he said, was to 'remake the world.' For us fairly innocent and naïve teenagers—fourteen, sixteen, and eighteen—that was pretty heady stuff.

"Dr. Buchman believed that change in the world begins with change in one's own life, 'walking the talk' in today's terminology. His approach to some of the most intractable problems of the age, such as the reconstruction of postwar Europe, made a lot of sense to us as well as to leaders of many countries who decorated him for his work in international relations following World War II. In the happy days of

At the Hamburg Zoo they tackled the dinosaur exhibit. "This is Ralph and me riding the dinosaur after having broken him," Paul wrote. "It was tough, as is all dinosaur breaking, but we love our work."

Trois bons copains

From Denmark they sent brother Ted a postcard of mules. "We thought we'd have a picture taken at one of those photo shops," they wrote. "Paul was a little disappointed. Says it makes his nose look longer than it really is."

In Italy they sang from a wagon in the village square for the families of cane workers at Torviscosa. One day Paul wrote home: "Thanks for sending on the royalty check. I'm sort of wondering if they put the decimal point in the right place."

the 1950s, there weren't that many opportunities, especially for young people, to be involved in matters beyond their personal worlds. It was the vision of making a relevant contribution and performing on a global stage that appealed to our youthful idealism and got us hooked.

"Dr. Buchman emphasized the importance of moral standards that are shared by the major faiths, and encouraged daily meditation to find a larger purpose for one's life, not just to be a better person but to make a difference in the community and the world. The appeal of being dedicated to a significant cause alongside this attractive group fired our young imaginations. The story of our adventures may not contain a lot of sexual escapades and drug experimentation, yet it might be said that the lifestyle we embraced, especially in the turbulent 1960s, was a true counterculture to the trends of those times.

"On our first visit to London," Ralph remembered, "we wrote a song that went like this."

> Let's go down and look around,
> A hillbilly is at home in London town.
> We're brothers and sisters from long ago,
> I know 'cause my grandaddy told me so.

In Copenhagen, they'd been hosted by Ole Bjorn Kraft, the former Danish foreign minister and NATO chairman, and appeared in a prestigious annual concert with opera and pop stars from several countries. They sang in Geneva for Russian and Chinese delegates to the International Labor Organization. In Italy, they sang for

thousands of textile workers and their families, and for exiled Queen Helen and King Michael of Romania and her sister, the Duchess of Aosta, in the duchess's secluded villa outside Florence.

In December, the brothers received an invitation that set them spinning. Buchman invited them to accompany him on a high-level tour of Asian nations. They would meet and sing for the heads of state of Sri Lanka, Japan, the Republic of China (Taiwan), the Philippines, Vietnam, Thailand, and Burma, and perform in scores of venues.

Buchman assembled an eclectic group of thirty for the tour, including an English colonel whose brother had been governor-general of Australia, the former Anglican bishop of Burma, a German prince who was a cousin of the Duke of Edinburgh, and the Colwells.

The tour began at Genoa on January 6, 1956 aboard the Italian liner SS *Surriento*. At Naples, Italians immigrating to Australia came aboard, serenaded by Neapolitan songs wafting up from the dockside in tearful farewell. At midnight, they passed the island of Stromboli, where one of the world's most active volcanoes is located. The crimson lava slashing down its sides was clearly visible in the blackness.

By daylight, they steamed through the Mediterranean to Port Said, the entrance of the Suez Canal. There, they waited several hours for other traffic to move through the canal.

"At about 3:00 a.m.," said Steve, "we were wakened by strange noises and shouts. We looked out and saw about a hundred Egyptians rowing around the ship in small boats, trying to sell the passengers everything from shoes to dates. They'd made sure everyone was awake by pounding on the hull!"

The first port of call would be Colombo, the capital of Sri Lanka, then called Ceylon. During the

They set out from Italy in January, 1956 aboard the SS *Surriento* at the start a nine-nation tour. They would perform for heads of state, in parliaments, and in hundreds of other venues. They would discover when they reached Australia just how close they had come to experiencing a very different kind of adventure.

The Surriento weighed anchor on a warm tropical night for a ten-day sail to Perth in Western Australia. Two days later, they felt a lurch and asked the captain about it. "We just went over the equator," he said.

lively ten-day trip, the brothers performed for the officers and crew, the cooks in the galley, and all who worked below decks. They wrote a song, "The Smiling Surriento," which was a big hit for the four hundred people packed into the ship's lounge. (Surriento means "smiling" in the Neapolitan dialect.)

The Ceylon visit was a twenty-two-hour marathon. Early in the morning, the prime minister's launch met the ship to take Buchman and his party ashore. At a mid-morning reception, the brothers performed a special song for Governor General Gunawardene. He requested an encore for his family and arranged for three broadcasts to be prepared later in the day for Radio Ceylon, which reached much of Southeast Asia. They sang in the early afternoon for cabinet ministers and parliamentarians—Muslim, Buddhist, and Hindu—and then for Prime Minister Bandaranaike, who insisted on having a copy of the words and music of "Sri Lanka," which the brothers had written and rehearsed until the small hours of the morning on the ship.

The *Surriento* weighed anchor on a warm tropical night for a ten-day sail to Perth in Western Australia. Two days later, they felt a lurch and asked the captain about it. "We just went over the equator," he said.

"Some of our friends were a bit shaken when we docked in Melbourne the next week and the authorities called for a safety inspection," Steve said. "They found that every lifeboat but one was rusted to the davits and wouldn't move. The one that reached the water quickly sank. The captain got a hefty fine."

In Melbourne, Sydney, and Canberra the Colwells sang for parliamentarians (in the Parliament itself in Canberra), met with the head of the 1956 Olympics, and performed on dozens of occasions. At informal and sometimes formal events, when speeches ended and it was time for a change of pace, they would hear Buchman call out "Bo-eeys!" in a voice that swept up at the end like a call for a party, and they would be on, frequently with a special song. As they never knew when that moment would come, they always kept their instruments with them, tuned and ready.

A trademark of Buchman's reconciliation work was having the people who traveled with him share their experiences and give firsthand accounts of problems being solved in their parts of the world. He'd then introduce the Colwells for a complete change of pace, perhaps a bluegrass number or their tongue-in-cheek "Isn't It Terribly Sad (That I'm So Good and the World's So Bad)?"

"If nothing else," Paul quipped, "we were always good for a few laughs."

Usually, the brothers were part of an occasion. But sometimes they were the occasion. Paul remembered an evening in the modest home of Ted Bull, the militant head of Australia's longshoremen's union that was threatening to close the nation's ports. They sang and talked through the evening. In the course of the conversation, they told him about their dad. Bull, whose ideological conviction usually put him in conflict with management, was intrigued to learn of an American who put people and integrity before profits.

In Sydney on April 24, Ralph completed the last of his high school studies. His brothers awarded him with an "Ornery Degree." Then, during a two-week visit to New Zealand, they sang for the king of the Maori people in the native language.

At the start of a whirlwind ten-day visit to Japan in mid-April, hundreds greeted the travelers at the airport, including leaders from the chief political parties, fresh from a violent debate in the Diet. Interest in Buchman's group was high, and the brothers sang at a string of events, including receptions by the governor of Tokyo, the governor of the Bank of Japan, and the minister of finance, plus a meeting with the leaders of the Seinendan, the four-million-member organization of Japanese rural youth.

On the fifth day of the visit, which was the emperor's birthday, the group had breakfast with Prime Minister Hatoyama and a collection of his children and grandchildren. They visited Parliament, where a bitter fight was raging in the lower house.

For his final two years of high school, Ralph studied on the road through a course from the University of Nebraska. In August, 1954 his friends gave him an 'offishal' certificate.

In Celebration of
The Birthday of His Majesty the Emperor
(of Japan)
Mr. Mamoru Shigemitsu
The Minister for Foreign Affairs
requests the pleasure of the company of
Mr. Stephen Colwell
at a Reception
on Sunday, April 29th, 1956, from 5.30 to 7.00 p.m.
at the Sori Kantei (Cabinet House),
Nagata-cho.

R.S.V.P.
Tel. 59-8510 57-8882

The brothers' host during a whirlwind ten-day visit to Japan was Taizo Ishizaka, chairman of Toshiba industries. They regularly sent mementos of their travels home, and Steve sometimes added notes to official invitations (so younger brother Ted would know just which emperor was being referred to).

The Socialists thought a bill being pushed by the government would deprive them of fifty seats. They had forced two all-night sessions and were planning a massive street protest the next day, which happened to be the first of May. The Conservatives, meanwhile, were talking of calling in police onto the Diet floor.

At a luncheon and the packed meeting that followed it, a different mood prevailed. Leading figures of both parties welcomed the travelers, who told of their struggles and the resolution of conflicts. The Colwells had everyone laughing, and provided a moving moment with the special song for Japan they had sung for the prime minister and his family. It expressed a vision for Japan in the future as "A Lighthouse of Asia" ("Nippon wa Ajia no Todai"). That same evening, at another event for Buchman's group, the ranking member of the majority party rushed in with news that the offensive bill had been sent back to committee. "Violence has been averted," he said.

The next stop was Taiwan, where the brothers learned a Chinese folk song called "Ding Hao!" ("Very Good!"), and added a funny, whimsical verse for Generalissimo Chiang Kai-shek, which delighted the Chinese leader.

In Manila, the only time the Philippines' charismatic president, Ramon Magsaysay, could carve out time for the visitors was over breakfast in Malaca-ang Palace. He was dealing then with the Huk Rebellion, led by a group of Marxist militants. His days were packed with meetings, negotiations, and talks with the rebels.

"The president was an extraordinary and courageous leader," Paul said, "determined to root out corruption, even to the extent of not allowing any of his family to hold a position in government. At one point, he went into the jungle alone unarmed to meet with the Huk rebels."

When Magsaysay invited Buchman to speak after the breakfast, the MRA leader said only one sentence, according to his longtime assistant Morris Martin, which was to give the president greetings from a Chinese cardinal they both knew. "Then he encouraged different ones of the party to tell of their experiences. An aide came and whispered in the president's ear, 'Time to go.' He was waved away, as the president was obviously intrigued by what he was hearing.

In Taiwan the brothers learned a folk song called "Ding Hao!" ("Very Good!"), and added an amusing verse for Generalissimo Chiang Kai-shek, which delighted the Chinese leader.

"Then the Colwells were asked to sing. They started off with a couple of country and western songs, then some original compositions, and then they sang a new song partly in Tagalog they'd written for the visit to the tune of an old Filipino folk tune: 'Pilipinas Mabuhay!' ('Long Live the Philippines!').

"The president was delighted. The aide approached and whispered again. 'Cancel the appointment,' said Magsaysay. Then he turned to Buchman: 'Let me have those three fellows with their music for a few months and we'll have no more trouble with the Huks!' Buchman said regretfully that he had plans for them. Magsaysay called back the aide to send for the Signal Corps to record the brothers so that their songs could be heard throughout the country. There were several encores before the breakfast ended."

"In Saigon," Steve said, "Vietnamese President Ngo Dinh Diem received us with all his cabinet and we sang at the university and at an orphanage and on the radio. We had a banquet and ate bird's nest soup, complete with the whole bird. I was bothered by it staring up at me, so I cut off its head and hid it under the edge of the plate. When the plate was cleared, there it was staring up at me again!

"Ralph set aside his bass to hold the Vietnamese words of a special song we'd written for the president. Two years later, when we came back to Saigon and again performed for President Diem and his family, there were banners strung across the boulevards to welcome our group. This time we wrote a new song. The 'hook' (in

In Saigon, Vietnamese President Ngo Dinh Diem and all his cabinet received the group. The first lady, Madam Nu, brought her son to hear the brothers play.

Vietnamese), was 'Long Live Vietnam'; in French, 'Pays des braves et des preux…Marche vers un jour glorieu.' Translated roughly, it means, 'Country of brave and proud people…march toward a glorious future.' Little did we know how events would unfold for this historic, tragic figure and his country.

"In Thailand, the prime minister, Field Marshal Pibulsonggram, who had been to Caux, met and garlanded each of us at the airport. He and his wife stayed with us past midnight, making sure we were taken care of."

But the work of the evening was just beginning, Steve noted. "We wanted to have a special song ready to sing to the prime minister, and the only time we had to produce it was that night, which wasn't all that unusual. We'd had other all-night sessions, and some were pretty funny. Ralph, who as the youngest was usually forgiven for it, tended to drop off to sleep. Paul would be wrestling for just the right thought to complete a couplet, when Ralph would suddenly open his eyes, come out with the perfect phrase, and then go right back to sleep! That night we just didn't have the energy to compose an original tune. So we dug back into our collective memories and came up with an old country song called 'Mexican Joe,' and wrote all new lyrics to it for Thailand. 'Mexican Joe' never had a more auspicious audience!"

"When we landed in Burma," Ralph said, "we were rushed immediately to Prime Minister U Nu's home. He had flown down from his summer residence in the hills to Rangoon so Dr. Buchman wouldn't have to make the difficult trip up to him. We learned it was the month of the twenty-five hundredth anniversary of the enlightenment of the Buddha. U Nu impressed us as having an inner quality, almost an inner glow that you don't see that often. It was an honor to meet him and sing for him in Burmese. We had written a special song: 'Bama Amiaji Kaunde' ('Burma Is the Ruby of the Orient'). U Thant, who would later become secretary general of the United Nations, was with the prime minister."

Early in May, four months after setting out, Steve, Paul and Ralph flew back to Rome via Karachi. They had been intensely affected by the tour, especially the last thirty days, when they had performed for a succession of heads of state and become the only musicians ever invited to perform in the Japanese Diet. "I'm sure we'll look back on this time as the highlight of our lives," Steve wrote from Rome.

They would fly back to the Philippines on the following April for a Pan-Asian conference that Ramon Magsaysay was to attend. "If those Colwell boys are going to be there," the president had said, "you can be sure I'll be there too." But a tragedy would intervene.

In Burma Prime Minister U Nu received the party on the twenty-five hundredth anniversary of the enlightenment of the Buddha. As in other countries, the group was given a gala banquet.

A happy Maori welcome in New Zealand.

In honor of Dr. Frank N. L. Buchman

MALACAÑANG

The President (of Philippines)

requests the pleasure of the company of

Mrs. J. Colwell

at Breakfast

on Saturday, May 5, 1956

at eight o'clock

Malacañang

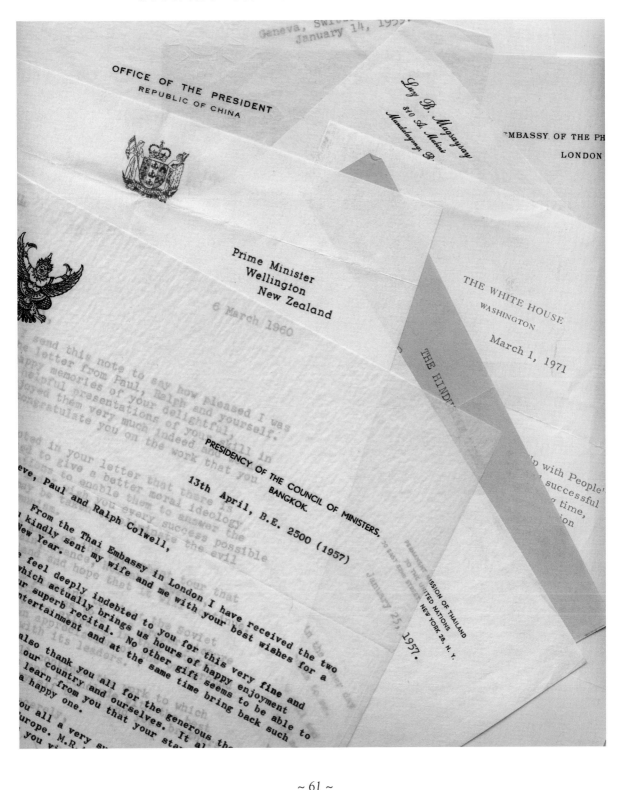

OFFICE OF THE PRESIDENT
REPUBLIC OF CHINA

Geneva, Swi...
January 14, 195...

Ray B. Magsaysay
810 A. Mabini
Mandaluyong, R...

...MBASSY OF THE PH...

LONDON

Prime Minister
Wellington
New Zealand

6 March 1960

THE WHITE HOUSE
WASHINGTON

March 1, 1971

PRESIDENCY OF THE COUNCIL OF MINISTERS,
BANGKOK.

13th April, B.E. 2500 (1957)

THE HIND...

...send this note to say how pleased I was
...he letter from Paul, Ralph and yourself.
...appy memories of your delightful still in
...helpful presentations of your...
...joyed them very much indeed a...
...congratulate you on the work that you...

...ted in your letter that there i...
...el to give a better moral ideology
...ion to enable them to answer the
...ay be ta...

...eve, Paul and Ralph Colwell,

...From the Thai Embassy in London I have received the two
...kindly sent my wife and me with your best wishes for a
...New Year.

...e feel deeply indebted to you for this very fine and
...which actually brings us hours of happy enjoyment
...ur superb recital. No other gift seems to be able to
...entertainment and at the same time bring back such
...with its leaders.

...also thank you all for the generous th...
...our country and ourselves. It al...
...learn from you that your sta...
...a happy one.
...ou all a very su...
...urope. M.R.L...
...you vi...

PERMANENT MISSION OF THAILAND
TO THE UNITED NATIONS
...E 38th STREET
NEW YORK 26, N. Y.

January 25, 1957.

...Up with People...
...successful...
...ion

Delegates to the Swiss conferences often requested photographs with Herb and the Colwells. The name and nationality of this gentleman from Africa regrettably was not retained, but Paul identified the bass fiddle as "George."

Herb and Dot Allen traveled to Switzerland to see their son in July 1955. They had not been on the same continent for years, and Steve wrote his parents that "Herb gets darn homesick and wants to see his family." It was a happy reunion. They were photographed with two of Herb's friends: Leland Holland, at rear, was the singing star of *Jotham Valley, The Good Road* and other musical productions. Tom Mboya, a young statesman from Kenya, was considered a possible successor to Jomo Kenyatta. Tragically, a Kikuyu tribesman assassinated Mboya in Nairobi in 1969.

"Pie in the Sky"

Paul Colwell and Bill Cates

Poor boy cries for a piece of the pie,
No shoes, dirty shorts,
Shirt half his size,
When the plate comes around
It is empty,
So he goes to bed to dream instead
Of a piece of bread,

> And pie dangling in the sky,
> Just beyond his fingertips,
> His hungry little body shakes.
> Pie dangling in the sky,
> It isn't fair, it lingers there,
> And before he can taste it
> He awakes.

Nothin' left but an empty shelf,
And the saying goes, "God helps those
Who help themselves."
So we helped ourselves
While there was plenty,
God help us now and please allow
Him more somehow,

> Then pie dangling in the sky,
> Just beyond his fingertips,
> His hungry little body shakes.
> Pie dangling in the sky,
> It isn't fair, it lingers there,
> And before he can taste it
> He awakes.

6

BITTERSWEET RETURN

A week before the 1957 Pan-Asian conference in the Philippines that the brothers were to attend, Ramon Magsaysay was killed in an air crash. The whole country mourned the loss of a beloved and effective leader. "Who knows how Asian history would have played out had he lived?" Paul said later. "He was a rare breed of statesman and I don't think there's ever been another like him."

At the gravesite of President Magsaysay, the brothers paid homage to their friend amid a sea of saddened Filipinos. His widow, Luz Magsaysay, requested a visit. "During a wonderful morning," wrote Steve, "she graciously received our whole group, and promised to be in touch with us soon so we could meet her son. A few days later, we were invited to her home. We arrived at 4 p.m., thought we'd only stay for tea, but didn't say good-bye until nearly 11.

"When Mrs. Magsaysay called for us to sing, we picked up our instruments and saw there were many more people there than the immediate family. There were cousins by the dozens, the son of the late secretary of education whose father was also killed in that plane crash, the general who heads the national police, the first lady's brother-in-law, and many friends who came in and out all evening.

"She kept us singing until we'd used almost every song in our repertoire, and we even sang some twice. We only paused from time to time, at her suggestion,

At the gravesite of President Magsaysay, amid a sea of saddened Filipinos, the brothers paid homage to their friend who had been killed only a week before in an air crash.

The President's widow asked for a visit from the international group, and later invited the Colwells to her home to sing for her family and friends.

In May the brothers sang in Japan at a send-off party for Prime Minister Kishi (right) as he set out on a grueling tour of Asian countries, where he openly apologized for Japanese atrocities during World War II.

for a Coke or 7UP. Just as we were wondering if it was time to go, she invited us for dinner. There we had a chance to tell her son, Jun, and his friends why we had left our budding music career and formal education in California to try to help bring about a more peaceful and just world."

At the beginning of May, the brothers returned to Japan. In his book, Inventing Japan-1853-1964 (Random House 2003), author/historian Ian Buruma, wrote: "One of the first things Kishi did when he became Prime Minister in 1957 was to go on a grueling tour of Southeast Asia where he apologized for the atrocities committed by the Japanese troops during the war." Kishi's tour made news across the world.

The Colwells and six of their friends were invited to the send-off party for this historic trip at Kishi's official residence. "We arrived at 8:45 p.m.," Steve wrote, "and were greeted by Diet member Hoshijima, who took us to a 'secret' room next to the reception hall where he gave us tea. He briefed us on the evening. Nothing else was scheduled, he said, and we were to have the whole program. He wanted songs and speakers.

"At 9:20, the prime minister arrived. Immediately, Hoshijima took the floor, spoke briefly, and introduced us. The room was lined with cabinet ministers, high government officials, Diet members, and Mrs. Kishi and the cabinet wives.

"Kishi smiled when he saw us and nodded his head; we had met him last year when

Dr. Buchman was received in the Diet, and we had performed the 'The Lighthouse for Asia' song for then-Prime Minister Hatoyama. This time, the song was interrupted several times by applause. There was a special verse for Kishi and his cabinet. This broke the ice. By this time the prime minister was beaming and moved closer so he could hear and see better. Next we sang another new song in Japanese that referred to Kishi's statement of the need for a humble heart, with a special verse about his upcoming tour.

"As the song finished, a few aides and secretaries began to get a little anxious and tried to herd the crowd into the next room for the official toast. Kishi would not budge. Then Masa Shibusawa spoke with great sincerity about the historic significance of this moment in the world, and moved the prime minister very much. Masa is highly respected; his family has been very influential in Japan for generations. By this time the secretaries were really determined, so we finished with 'Masuguni,' a song we'd written with Hideo Nakajima based on Kishi's vision for Japan, which was to go not to the left, or the right, but straight (hidare demu naku, mingi demu naku ...). The prime minister came up and greeted each of us and thanked us warmly. After the toast he came back to shake hands and thank us again."

The Colwell family visited their globetrotting sons in Japan during the country's annual Cherry Blossom Festival. Prime Minister and Mrs. Kishi welcomed them at the official reception.

~

The Colwells urgently needed a break. They had been on tour practically nonstop for four years, not just one "world tour," but many. The break would be in Karuizawa, a mountain resort about three hours from Tokyo, where leading families of the capital go to escape the summer heat. The change of pace was a godsend for Paul. "Just after arriving, I had a bad asthma attack and was laid up for more than a week. It turned out that I was quite run-down and this was the perfect place to build up for the months ahead. I've had lots of air, exercise and rest, and am even learning golf, in case it might be useful one day with Kishi or Ike!"

One afternoon in Karuizawa, the brothers serenaded Princess Chichibu. Her late husband, who died of TB in 1953, was heir-apparent to the Emperor.

Initially, Steve felt a different emotion. "To be honest, taking that kind of a break gave me some insecurity. We had been on the move so constantly, so tightly scheduled, that when we didn't have that, I felt a sort of vacuum."

When Paul and Ralph were younger, Steve was the gyroscope that held the compass steady. Being a "group" of brothers and performers committed to major goals was far more challenging than being three individuals hanging around together.

In Karuizawa, people whose schedules in Tokyo were jammed with urgent affairs were able to set their own priorities. On three occasions, the Colwells were invited to the home of the head of N.H.K., Japan's largest radio and TV network. "His family knows our music now," Ralph said, "and everyone sings along with us. He's asked us to perform on his stations as we travel through Japan this fall."

"Hideo Nakajima, our talented friend and colleague, has been our lyrics collaborator in all our Japanese material while we've been here," Paul said. "He's a brilliant wordsmith and we consider him one of us kiodas (brothers). He has quite a story. He was trained as a human torpedo during the war. 'But I'm here,' he always says with a big smile, 'because the war ended and I didn't go off!'"

Steve said: "Some of our Japanese friends invited us to be in a tennis tournament. It was a mixed doubles event. Not knowing any other players, I was paired with a lady, Japanese of course, whom I had never met, let alone played tennis with. We lost on the third round to a team that included Michiko, the future wife of

Crown Prince Akihito, who went on to play the crown prince and his partner. I don't know who won that day, but I do know it was a good match; and I truly believe that because I lost in that third round to Michiko I was responsible for their meeting."

The brothers worked for the rest of the year with the Seinendan organization, which included the majority of farming youth of Japan, touring with *Road to Tomorrow*, a stage play the young Japanese had written at Mackinac.

The Colwells traveled by train in South India. The journeys continued all through the decade and into the next, an education in all probability without parallel.

On March 4, 1958, Ralph wrote home: "As our ferry boat got closer to Hiroshima, I began to feel real fear about going there. It's one thing to discuss the atom bomb from thousands of miles away, but being here was another matter. The reality of it gripped me. More confused than guilty, I thought to myself that the quicker we got out of there, the better. It was something too big for me to handle. I think I felt afraid to face the people squarely. Then I thought, remember why we've come; we're here because we're building for the future.

"Our songs were received in Hiroshima just as enthusiastically as anywhere else. It's a lovely modern city now, with the widest streets of any city in Japan. On the memorial in the Peace Park at the city center is an inscription placed there by former Mayor Hamai, who was deeply affected by his visit to Caux a number of years ago. It reads: 'Sleep peacefully. We shall not make the same mistake again.'"

During Japan's annual cherry blossom festival in April, the senior Colwells and Ted traveled to Tokyo for a fortnight visit with their globetrotting sons. At fourteen, Ted was learning to play the fiddle, with the prospect of adding more bluegrass flavor to the band. It was a happy reunion; the famous cherry trees were bursting into springtime glory, and pictures were taken of the family with Prime Minister and Mrs. Kishi at the official festival reception. The family visit gave everyone the chance to express things that none of them had been inclined to write in letters. Ted went along with the brothers a month later when they paid a return visit to Taiwan, then returned home.

By May, the trio had reached India, where they sang for the mayor of Bombay, the country's top filmmaker in Madras, and the American ambassador in New Delhi. President Rajendra Prasad received them at his summer residence in Simla. The city is a coveted mountain resort, and Ralph, Paul, and a few friends gained permission to ride the magnificent horses of the government stable.

Paul's letter home about the Simla visit ended in typical style: "This place is 7,000 feet up in the foothills of the Himalayas, like the Lake Arrowhead of India without the lake."

In Simla the governor and chief of police gave the Colwells and few friends permission to exercise their horses. Ralph wrote brother Ted: "The horses were very obedient except for the one I had on the last day. When I got in the saddle at the police stables, the guy said quietly, 'Strong horse.' I soon found out."

Singing in Florida Blanca, a town north of Manila (left).

Colleague Stewart Lancaster, bass fiddle-bearer, Indian style (below).

"Till Everyone is Home"

Paul and Ralph Colwell, Herb Allen

The beauty of life shines around you,
Like the sun breaking through a storm that has been.
But sometimes you can't see the rainbow
If you feel like a stranger
On the outside looking in.

I can see some flowers in the window
Of a tiny one room shack
Nestled on a hill.
Nothing can hold down the power
Of a hope that keeps growing,
And you know it always will.

> *Till everyone is home,*
> *Till everyone is home,*
> *Till the last soul is fed*
> *And there's a roof above his head.*
> *As long as there's someone*
> *Left out in the cold,*
> *As long as there's someone*
> *Without a place to call his own,*
> *How can there be peace,*
> *How can we be free to lay down the load?*
> *We're still on the road*
> *Till everyone, till everyone is home.*

7
LAND FOR THE PEOPLE

The cover of *Time* magazine on May 11, 1953 featured a portrait of India's beloved and bespectacled Vinoba Bhave over a caption that read, "I have come to loot you with love." Since the start of the decade, Vinoba had been walking through the nation, village by village. His mission was to obtain land, voluntarily given, for the poor. A "Robin Hood by request," declared one dumbfounded observer, Vinoba was a devoted disciple of Mahatma Gandhi and had endured nearly five years in prison during India's struggle for independence. The world regarded him as Gandhi's successor, and his spiritual stature was enormous.

The throngs who turned out to hear their beloved Vinoba Bhave, venerated as the successor to India's Mahatma Ghandi, were surprised to see three Hollywood cowboys complete with western hats and a big bass fiddle. Ghandi's grandson, Rajmohan, is at left.

The Colwell brothers were in Simla in 1958 when they received Vinoba's invitation to join him in Maharashtra state, fifteen hundred miles to the south. "We were astounded and honored," Paul said.

Six would make up the party: Rajmohan Gandhi, who was Mahatma Gandhi's grandson and who had arranged the invitation; Keeku Gandhi, a Parsi who shared the Gandhi name but was not related; journalist Stewart Lancaster; and the brothers.

The trek from Simla began by bus and train, and continued from Delhi to Bombay by plane. "Waiting in Bombay for the train to Poona, which is the second

At four thirty in the morning Vinoba set out at a brisk pace down the road, bound for the next village. About eighty of us followed behind. As it was still dark, two men carrying lanterns flanked Vinoba, and a third lantern bearer walked ahead.

largest city in the state," Steve wrote, "who should we meet but Senator Rajabhoj, a friend of Rajmohan's, who helped us compose a song in Marathi. Marathi is Vinoba's mother tongue and the language of Maharashtra state. The song title in English meant, 'There's enough land in the world for everyone's need, but not enough for everyone's greed.'"

Steve's matter-of-fact notation about writing a song while waiting for a train in a Bombay railway station in a language they'd never heard before belies the improbability of the feat. They could do it because they'd been creating on the run in a similar manner for five years; they would also practice for hours during the balance of the trip to be ready to perform the song.

"Poona is 120 miles southeast of Bombay," Steve continued, "and we arrived at eight in the evening of May 21st. Standing on the platform, the question was, how do we find Vinoba? He was in a different village every day. Keeku suggested we ask Mrs. Mehta, an old friend of the Mahatma who lived just down the road, and she gave us the answer. She welcomed us warmly and took us into the room where Gandhi had often stayed. It was kept just as he had left it. We sat on the floor there and discussed our next step, which turned out to be a well-worn seven-seater Plymouth that had celebrated its twentieth birthday. At 4:30 a.m., our chauffeur, Sheikh Mohammed, a nonpraying Muslim, packed us in beside Ralph's bass, cranked up the old Plymouth, and took us streaking through the early hours of the morning, skillfully dodging bullock carts and goat herds.

"Rajmohan navigated by aid of road map, intuition, and determination. He estimated a distance of 180 miles southeast of Poona, and our expected arrival at noon; it was actually 3 p.m. We had not taken into account the need to stop every twenty-five miles to cool our panting Plymouth, nor the fording of numerous rivers. The highway was paved every so often for the first hundred miles. The rest, according to the road map, was 'subject to weather conditions.' The river crossings were a refreshing interlude to the hot, dusty drive. Once, as we waded in to find the shallowest path for the car to cross, Lancaster seized the chance to wash his socks Indian-style, beating them on a rock.

"Breakfast was had in a small village eighty miles out of Poona in a mud-hut restaurant under a banyan tree. The proprietor proudly welcomed us to his home, taking us from room to roof to family shrine. In one room he showed us a picture of Gandhi and was thrilled to learn who Rajmohan was.

"Ten and a half hours out of Poona, we arrived at a small school on the out-skirts of the village of Atpari. Three cowboys and a bass fiddle appearing caused quite a sensation. But Vinoba's secretary was the most excited, as the telegram we had sent from Poona announcing our arrival had not yet reached him. The people of the village took us immediately to the big well where we washed. The ladies laid out a special meal on banana leaves and we ate sitting on the floor. We were told that Vinoba wanted to see us at 4:30 p.m.

"When the time came, we were taken to a large room. Surrounded by about fifty of his workers, Vinoba sat cross-legged, propped up by a large pillow, dressed Gandhi-style. His uncombed beard, almost entirely white, strengthened his appearance as the arche-typal holy man, although he certainly did not intend it. He wore round glasses, with yellow plastic frames and large half-moon bifocal lenses. Before him was a small table on which he was working on trans-

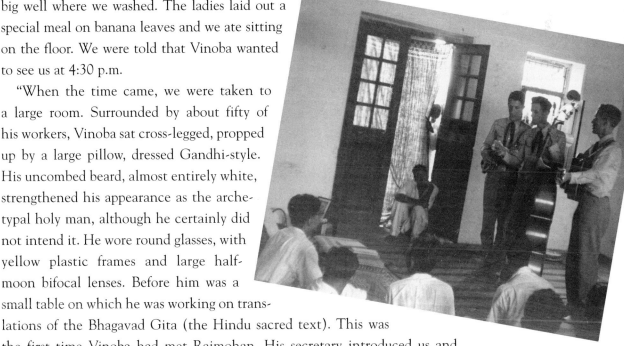

"We sang for Vinoba, introduced by Rajmohan Gandhi, Mahatma Gandhi's grandson, who we were traveling with. Vinoba especially liked the song we had written in the Marathi language for him, and used it as the theme of his talk to the crowd that evening, 'There's enough land in the world for everyone's need.'"

lations of the Bhagavad Gita (the Hindu sacred text). This was the first time Vinoba had met Rajmohan. His secretary introduced us and asked what we would like to do. Our only thought was to sing. We began with the Hindi song we had written for the president of India. Initially, we couldn't see Vinoba's reaction behind his beard. Then we did the new song we had written in Marathi for him. That he really liked. We sang more, and soon he was moving to the rhythm. He's a bit hard of hearing, so Rajmohan repeated the important lines for him.

"Vinoba then motioned for us to sit around him. He was aware of what we'd been doing. 'You are moving all over the world on a goodwill mission which is absolutely necessary,' he told us. 'Unfortunately the world is divided into so many nations which are afraid of each other without any reason.' He said the world needs building on nonviolent and truthful lines. 'So I am hoping that you and men like me, who are working in the same field, namely of inculcating non-violence, all form a big moral block against nothing less than the evil that is not merely outside but is within us. I congratulate you, bless you, and thank you.'

"Meanwhile, out on the hockey field, crowds were gathering for the 5:30 meeting. Vinoba rose and instructed the secretary to have us take the first half-hour of the meeting, and to be sure to have us sing the song in Marathi. Ten thousand villagers in bright colored turbans were sitting on the ground eagerly waiting to hear the great man. You can imagine their wide-eyed wonderment when the grandson of Mahatma Gandhi was introduced to them, accompanied by three cowboys and the bass fiddle.

"At six o'clock, as we sang the last refrain of our song about the land, Vinoba quietly mounted the raised platform behind us. There was a great cheer from the people and then a hush. Fathers and sons in the center, mothers and daughters on the side listened for 'Baba's' message for them. He took our song as the theme of his talk—'there's enough land in the world for everybody's need,' and 'if everyone cares enough and shares enough, everyone will have enough.' He had the audience laughing heartily when he joked about the size of Ralph's bass fiddle. He said, 'These boys come with songs of love and understanding. We also have songs like these in India.' And he began to sing. He challenged them to respond to our message by demonstrating love and unity among themselves and by sharing their land. When the meeting ended, young and old swarmed around us; we made many friends. Suddenly the sky broke open into a rainstorm, and the villagers said it was a sign, a good omen that we had come. All this was way beyond us, that Vinoba included us as he did. We felt greatly honored.

"Next was supper prepared by the village ladies. At eight o'clock we joined in the evening prayers in Vinoba's room. Vinoba led the Hindu hymns and the others joined in vigorously.

"They opened up the science room of the school, which was to be our quarters for the night. It wasn't the first time we had slept in a science room! Our bed consisted of a sheet of canvas spread out on the concrete floor. At 3 a.m. singing— the traditional alarm clock of Vinoba's camp—awakened us. At 3:30 there were morning prayers, and at 4:30 Vinoba set out at a brisk pace down the road, bound for the next village. About eighty of us followed behind. As it was still dark, two men carrying lanterns flanked Vinoba, and a third lantern bearer walked ahead. Chanting and the beating of drums caused us to turn around and, much to our amazement, we saw three Japanese Buddhist monks, who had

Time out for a coconut milk break at the Hindu shrine, Mahabalipuran, near Madras.

arrived at midnight from Gandhi's ashram, bringing up the rear and making the 'music.' It was all like a dream. There, a few paces ahead of us, was Vinoba wearing a loincloth and a shawl over his head and shoulders, exactly like the pictures we had seen of Gandhi. Dawn was just breaking and across the fields came the singing of the farmers as they drove their bullocks.

"Our arrival into the village of Dighanchi was an experience never to be forgotten. Thousands of people lined the street. Men blew large, curved buffalo horns as we approached the brightly decorated archway of welcome. The women held out burning incense. Beautifully colored patterns and designs had been drawn on the road leading through the village up to the schoolhouse where the new camp was made. The villagers joined the procession and seated themselves on the ground outside the school.

"…Vinoba had some of his people learn the words and music of our special song in Marathi about the land, so that it could be sung in all the villages. With that, we jumped into our trusty, dusty Plymouth, which was waiting for us at the village, and forded the river where many of Vinoba's team were washing their clothes. They all stopped to cheer and wave us off. From there on, it was 180 miles in a breezy 115-degree heat back to Poona."

"Save the Dancer"

Frank Fields, Ken Ashby,
Paul and Ralph Colwell, Steve Cornell

The ravages of human history,
The savageness of our sword,
Are as much of our legacy
As the heights we have explored.
It seems our questing for paradise
Is dressed in paradox,
Grownups playing with power
Like children playing with blocks.
But through the triumph and the tragedy,
Rising like a bird,
Is a dancer always dancing,
A dancer always dancing
To a tune we've never heard,
Save the dancer!

8

INTO AFRICA

The brothers seldom took time to evaluate the uniqueness of their life, let alone their lives. Their passports were studded with visas from around the world. Family communication, in spite of best intentions, was often problematical.

On July 14, 1958, after flying from India to Switzerland via London, Steve wrote his father on Paul Sr.'s fifty-first birthday: "Happy Birthday, Dad. Now you're just one year over the halfway mark! But it's also like a birthday for us too, because just this morning we received your good letter of May 3rd that you sent here, but for some reason went back to Asia and then to Mackinac and then finally back here to Caux! In the same package were Mother's letters to Ralph and Paul."

"Of course we got discouraged at times," Ralph said later. "But fortunately, that didn't happen to all of us at once; the others were there to help things get back on track." Their letters home minimized any wear and tear on their psyches or their bodies; they'd been dealing with those challenges all their lives. Steve had begun stuttering at age four, Ralph survived polio at thirteen, and Paul had struggled with serious asthma since childhood. But no matter how dedicated they were or how positive they maintained their attitudes, the traveling and distance took a toll.

Steve hadn't realized he stuttered until his early teens, when he had to memorize a poem and recite it for his ninth grade class. He'd worked then

They traveled to Stanger, a city in the province of Natal, to the home of Chief Albert Luthuli, who was president-general of the African National Congress (ANC). Luthuli had been "banned" by the government, and placed under house arrest. A year later Luthuli would become the first African to receive the Nobel Peace Prize.

The brothers had the use of a '57 Chevy during part of their South African visit.

with a speech therapist for two years, and his mother told him stuttering ran in the family. But it never interfered with his performances, and friends regarded any hesitation in conversation more as an element of his charm than as a problem.

Steve wrote from Caux in mid-August: "Paul arrived yesterday with all his bags from Dr. Oltramare's house in Geneva. (Daniel Oltramare, a leading Swiss physician, had been treating Paul's asthma without charging a fee since the brothers arrived in Europe in 1953.) He's looking and feeling great, but the doctor wants him to sing and work just three days a week for a while and be outdoors and rest the other four. He got here just in time to help us send off the Lord Abbot of the chief Buddhist monastery in Thailand, who's a cabinet minister and leads 200,000 monks."

At the end the month, Paul wrote to thank his parents for a parcel they'd sent for his twenty-fifth birthday. He listed the contents, including the "homemade cookies for young revolutionaries." But he said the gift that touched him most was a tape recording (reel-to-reel) of country songs. "That stopped everything. We listened to half of it yesterday with some friends including a Scottish concert violinist who has picked up a bit of country-style fiddling!

"There was a party for me in the afternoon, and the twenty-two students from Somaliland who are here came. Their leader is the president of the Somali students in Italy (Somaliland is an Italian colony that will be independent in 1960). They sang a crazy, fun song for me, a take-off on one we'd written for Africa. All of them are Muslim."

Two weeks later, Paul wrote that he was "laid up with another bronchial infection accompanied by some asthma, although much lighter than the last time. It gets sort of exasperating, but Dr. Oltramare came up yesterday and seems very encouraged by my progress. Thinking back, every attack I've had in the past five years I'm sure was caused by an infection. So we're advancing."

Don Saul was with the brothers and Herb in Denmark in the fall of 1953. "We were the guests of a friend in Copenhagen when Paul had a serious attack. We laid him out on our host's billiard table after the doctor had been called, and that's where he was when the doctor came. I'm sure Paul would remember that. Or maybe not; he's had a lot of attacks through the years."

"I was often very concerned about him," Steve said. "At times he had to sit on the edge of his bed all night with his hands on his knees, as it was the most comfortable position to get his breath. Many times I stayed with him and rubbed his back, which seemed to help. I learned how to give him shots by practicing on oranges. Sometimes I had to give him shots every day. In the spirit of 'the show must go on,' there were performances when Paul could hardly catch his breath, let alone sing. Ralph and I covered for him, and I don't think anyone in the audiences knew what was really going on. Paul battled bravely and seemed to accept this lifelong problem with his usual trademark, self-effacing humor. He was always making witty *sotto voce* comments. I don't ever remember him wanting to give in to his asthma or wanting to quit because of it. The cold and dampness of England and the winters in Europe were especially hard on him."

Whenever it was possible, a few days in a friendlier climate would be carved out of the band's schedule to provide a degree of relief and refreshment. One summer when their parents came to Europe, True Colwell joined Paul at a spa in France where he spent several weeks trying to overcome a serious skin infection.

While the European climate was not ideal for Paul's health, the humanity and human climate of Caux was a plus. Every summer the brothers and Allen reconnected there with friends from around the world. They produced music and theatrical productions, and took part with delegates in operating the center; it wasn't unusual to be on a wash-up crew with a British industrialist or a student from Japan. That December, with an African trip on the horizon, they helped famed French philosopher/author Gabriel Marcel introduce a new book, *Fresh Hope for the World*, in Paris. They were the ideal promotion for the launch, as Marcel had written an entire chapter about them.

In January 1959 the Colwells were invited to visit the African continent with an international team. They set out from Montreux, two thousand feet below Caux, eager to work in a new country, a new continent, and, for them, a new world. The tour began in South Africa, where civic officials, tribal

In January 1959 the Colwells were invited to visit the African continent with an international team. They set out for South Africa by train from Montreux, two thousand feet below Caux. The six-month visit would include Eastern and Western Cape Provinces, the Transkei, Johannesburg, and Natal.

chiefs, and the national press welcomed them. The six-month visit would include Eastern and Western Cape Provinces, the Transkei, Johannesburg, and Natal.

Apartheid, the government's policy of racial separation since 1948, was then in full force, yet with their music, the Colwells crossed social, tribal, and cultural divides. Doors opened everywhere. They performed at receptions and meetings with provincial and national figures at the seat of Afrikaner (people of Dutch and Huguenot descent) power in Pretoria, and traveled to Stanger, a city in the province of Natal, to the home of Chief Albert Luthuli, who was president-general of the African National Congress (ANC). Luthuli had been "banned" by the government, and placed under house arrest. Nelson Mandela, the future leader of the country, was then deputy president of the ANC.

"Meeting Chief Luthuli was a memorable experience," Steve said. "He was a highly educated man of deep Christian faith and at the forefront of resistance to the system that was suppressing his people. I remember how he responded when we sang for him in the garden of his home. I don't recall what he said, but I will never forget his face." The following year, Luthuli would become the first African to receive the Nobel Peace Prize.

One sun-filled Thursday morning in late April, Steve, Paul, and Ralph stood in their shirtsleeves atop a windswept promontory on the southern-most tip of the continent. The latitude there corresponded roughly to that of Atlanta and Los Angeles in the northern hemisphere and, as the seasons were correspondingly reversed, it was early fall. They were with George Daneel, an important figure in the groundswell of reform in the country. Daneel had become famous as a Springbok rugby star in the 1920s and was a *dominee* (minister) in the Dutch Reformed Church, which, in the words of biographer Mary Lean, made him "preeminent in both of Afrikanerdom's religions."

Daneel was one of the first Christian ministers to speak out against apartheid, forty-five years before his church would formally agree with his stance. Years earlier, in the 1930s, he had relinquished the bitterness he felt toward the English; Afrikaner-English hostility divided South Africa even before hostility between black and white. The brothers had initially met Daneel in Switzerland, and seen the respect African leaders who had been at Caux afforded him.

At lunch that day, Steve asked Daneel about Dr. William Nkomo, who sometimes spoke alongside him at meetings. "William is a remarkable man," Daneel answered. "We first met at MRA's Lusaka, Northern Rhodesia (now Zambia) conference in 1953, which was one of the first multiracial gatherings ever held in Southern Africa. All the delegates were there as equals. You know, my parents were devout Christians, but during that weekend I realized that when our servants came in for family prayers, they had to sit on the floor."

The affront of such superiority then dawned on him, he said. "It was not just a wrong relationship, it was a sin against God." Daneel apologized publicly to the black people who were present at the conference. One of them was Nkomo, the first president of the radical Youth League of the ANC. The brothers had heard Nkomo tell how he had renounced violence, convinced that his people would be served better by negotiation because "… it was more revolutionary to change people than to liquidate them."

Earlier, William and Mrs. Nkomo had invited the Colwells to their home in a township near Johannesburg. "It seemed as though the whole neighborhood was packed into the house that evening," Paul said. "They kept us going song after song."

The international team was welcomed across the spectrum of South African life. "In Johannesburg," Ralph said, "we gained special permission to hold multiracial meetings, in spite of them being illegal under apartheid." At Fort Hare, the country's only all-African university and a hotbed for nationalist agitation, they spoke and sang, and were surrounded by students afterwards for discussions about the burning issues of the day. Manasseh Moerane, the former president of the African Teachers Association of South Africa, introduced them in the schools of Port Elizabeth.

On the southernmost tip of the African continent with George Daneel, a pioneer in the struggle for racial equality in South Africa. Daneel was a minister in the Dutch Reformed Church and a star on the country's Springbok rugby team in the 1920s, which made him "preeminent in both of Afrikanerdom's religions."

Although apartheid was the absolute law of the land, Philip Vundla, a militant radical who had abandoned hatred, invited the Colwells into his township to perform. They played in schools, homes, and meeting centers in the Xhosa and Zulu languages. Vundla introduced them to a man who had once tried to kill him because of his changed attitude, but who now worked with him. In Cape Town, the family of Julian Sonn introduced them into the Coloured (mixed-race) community of the country. They rode horseback on the vast acreage of the Kingwill Ranch, hosted by the family of English heritage who grazed sheep on the arid plains of the Karoo. In Pretoria, they were houseguests of South Africa Supreme Court Justice Cornelis "Claassie" Claassen and his wife, Marie.

"Judge Claassen was highly respected," Paul said, "and he definitely broke ranks with his fellow Afrikaners when he suggested that they needed to make amends for the history of white domination of the African population." The brothers enjoyed the Claassen's three sons, Gert, Roger, and Neels. Gert and Roger would later work with them in Up with People, and Neels would take part in the all-African Sing Out, *Springbok Stampede*. When Nelson Mandela became president after the 1994 national elections, Gert became chief operating officer of the South African Broadcasting Corporation. Roger and Neels, both lawyers, became Supreme Court judges.

"Apartheid was so entrenched," Paul said, "its historical roots so deep, you felt that any chance of its being overturned lay with the white population in whose hands were all the cards and all the political and physical power—the Nationalist Party, in particular, which consisted primarily of Afrikaners. While we were there, we knew many who were reconsidering their position such as Justice Claassen and his family who courageously took a stand for change at some personal and professional cost.

"One leading Dutch Reformed clergyman whom we had come to know at a Caux conference and with whom we had a very intense conversation about South Africa was one of those reconsidering his whole concept of white supremacy. He made a speech at the conference that was picked up by the national news media at home. In his talk, he expressed his regret for the inhumanity inflicted on blacks in his country and suggested that some changes were needed in the system. It was a start in the right direction. However, upon his return to South Africa he came under such attack from his own people that he retracted the statements he made in Europe. It was obvious to us that this was going to take a long time.

"After six months in South Africa, we certainly didn't have any answers. We only knew that our music had perhaps had the effect of opening the hearts of people and the doors to homes and communities across the whole racial spectrum. Most important, it was an education for us and opened our hearts to the people of a continent where we would experience some of the most profound and meaningful times of our lives."

With long-time associate Al Cook they visited a gold mine in Johannesburg. Cook worked with the brothers for years in several countries.

At the end of the tour, the brothers and their good friend Al Cook from Canada visited South Africa's Kruger Park Game Preserve as guests of the manager.

One day as they were coming around a blind curve on one of the park's single-track dirt roads, they nearly ran into an elephant trotting toward them. Paul was driving and slammed on the brakes. The elephant slammed on its brakes. Paul rammed the car into reverse (claiming there were three other pairs of hands on the gearshift) and sped backward down the road. The elephant flapped its ears (not necessarily a good sign) and, much to their relief, ran off into the bush.

In Southern Rhodesia's Wankie Game Park, they were once again lucky to get out in one piece when they drove through a herd of elephants and got between a mother and her babies—an absolute no-no in Africa.

On their brief swing through Southern Rhodesia, later to become Zimbabwe, they sang original songs in Chibemba, Chinyanja, and Sindebele, three of the region's major languages.

In May, 1959 they were received by the mayor of Salisbury (the future Harare), Southern Rhodesia's capital, and then flew north across the continent, across rain forests, vast savannas, verdant valleys, and sand. In June,

On the Kingwill Ranch, where thousands of sheep grazed on the arid plains of the Karoo, they rode horseback and occasionally posed for pictures as genuine, immaculately dressed Hollywood cowhands.

they were back in Switzerland, and worked through the summer at the Caux conference center. There, Greek and Turkish Cypriots asked them to come before the end of the year to Cyprus, the small but strategic Mediterranean island that was about to gain its independence.

They were in Italy in the fall at the invitation of government officials. Ralph wrote his parents from Florence:

"I sent you a letter yesterday and forgot to tell you the most important news, which is: ahem—I've bought a new bass fiddle! Yep, there it is. Old George, with his chips and rattles and scratches and split parts and gashes and squeaks just couldn't take it any more. It all started last birthday, when friends pitched in to give me money for a new bass. A Danish fellow came up with 300 Swiss francs and some folks down in South Africa chipped in a few hundred francs and before long I was in the bass-buying business.

"I didn't have much of a chance to do any shopping until after the conference finished. Then a friend of George Fraser in Bern put us on to a guy in Lausanne who put us on to a guy in Geneva who makes violins and guitars for Andres Segovia. Over the phone on the day before we came down here to Italy, the Geneva guy told me he had a bass to sell. Paul and I promptly drove down there and came face to face with George Jr. (not George Fraser Jr.!). The Geneva guy had it made in Germany about five years ago. It's a ¾ size, just a fraction smaller than my original one, made out of pine and maple, and looks as good as new because it has been sitting around a radio studio its whole life and mostly been used in symphony orchestras. It has a good, refined, long note that carries very nicely. It's definitely more delicate than George Sr., so I'm determined to be a lot more careful.

"So that's that. We were hoping to find an American-made bass, but the Geneva guy said there ain't no such thing in Europe."

"Give the Children Back Their Childhood"

Paul Colwell, Herb Allen, Derek Gill

Give the children back their childhood,
Let the children run and play,
Don't make them fight your battles,
They're the ones who always seem to pay.
Don't make battlefields of their playgrounds,
Don't barricade their streets,
Or they'll grow up too soon
And they won't grow up complete.

Give the children back their childhood,
Let the children run and play
And skip away on wings of fantasy
And dream of what they'll be some day.
Don't feed their minds
With your bitter lines
And the prejudice that is yours.
And they just may
Forget some day
To carry on our wars.

9

ON CYPRUS WITH
THE GUERRILLAS

A Cypriot shepherd in the hills above Nicosia.

S teve writes (November 1959): "Paul, Ralph and I are here in Nicosia, Cyprus along with fifteen others of our international team. Greek and Turkish Cypriots we met at Caux invited us to come. We three may not be here for long, because we're supposed to go back to Africa.

"This exotic chunk of Mediterranean real estate has been traded back and forth between empires for centuries: Egyptian, Roman, Byzantine, Venitian, Ottoman, and more. It became a British Crown Colony in 1925, and five years ago was made headquarters of Britain's Middle East Command. A year later the insurgency began. The British declared a State of Emergency and brought in 40,000 troops during the peak of the fighting. Three fourths of the population here is Greek. The guerrillas, called the EOKA, are fighting for 'Enosis,' which would make Cyprus part of Greece. The Turkish Cypriots are bitterly opposed and civil war has been the result. But a treaty that guarantees Cyprus's independence was signed in London last January. The actual independence date is scheduled for next January, just five weeks away. We don't know if we'll still be here then, but we'd sure like to be.

"Archbishop Makarios heads the Greek Orthodox Church here. He will become president after the independence under the terms of the London treaty. The vice-president will be Dr. Fazil Kuchuk, the leader of the Turkish

community. In his home in Nicosia, Makarios receives us. He's an impressive
figure in his flowing beard, long black vestments and tall headpiece. He has
a long history of struggling for the Greeks of this island. They say that years
ago he secretly arranged for the creation of the EOKA guerillas. The British
deported him. But when the Archbishop changed his position last year and
agreed to Cyprus becoming an independent country, it opened the door to a
peaceful solution. How peaceful remains to be seen. Makarios listens atten-
tively to our delegation, and we sing for him in our best Greek.

"Sir Hugh Foot, the British governor, gives us a reception. He keeps us for
nearly an hour, and talks with us about all that needs to happen here. We sing
'Listen to the Lion Roar,' a song we'd written for Britain, with a special verse
for him. Then he shows us around the beautiful Governor's Mansion, and says
again and again that he'll see us on many other occasions, and that he definitely
wants us on the island doing our stuff. We'd like to stay.

"After the reception our friend Polycarpos Georgadjis, who's the minister of
labor in the Transitional Cabinet, picks up the three of us. He was a leader of
the EOKA guerillas, and we got to know him last summer at Caux. In his personal car Georgadjis drives us up into the Troodos Mountains. On the way we
stop by the home of an old EOKA friend of his. The man isn't there but his
parents are, a wonderful couple, salt of the earth. As if to prove that Cypriot
hospitality is about the best in the world, the old lady sits us down and in less
than ten minutes has us eating a huge lunch. (We had already had lunch, of
course. It is 3:30 in the afternoon!) In gratitude we sing our Greek song for
them, without instruments, and they really love it, especially the part about
'Long Live Makarios!' Stuffed, we say our goodbyes, pile back into the car, and
head on into the mountains.

"Mr. Georgadjis shows us the areas where he was hiding out, surrounded by
British troops.

"For how long, we ask?

"Sometimes for months at a time.'

"How did you survive?"

"We live here.'

"We wind higher and higher up the dirt road, but don't get the full view, as
there are lots of clouds. The highest peak in the Troodos range is 6400 ft, and

the terrain is rugged for miles around it. Most of the EOKA fighting took place here. All the way along we visit with Georgadjis, who is twenty-eight years old. He talks about the history of the island, the struggle from the standpoint of the Greek Cypriots, and the integrity needed now to assure effective leadership. Georgadjis is a national hero, and absolutely everyone knows and respects him. He expresses his appreciation for our being here during this critical period of transition.

Polycarpos Georgadjis, the Minister of Labor in the Transitional Cabinet, drove the brothers high into the Troodos Mountains and showed them where he and other EOKA guerillas had hidden for months, surrounded by British troops. During the insurgency Greek and Turkish Cypriots fought each other, and both fought the British.

"On Sunday, Rauf Denktash, the No. 2 man in the Turkish community, takes some of us into the country, first, to see the new villages being built by Turks whose homes had been destroyed by the Greeks, and second, to accompany Dr. Fazil Kuchuk, future vice-president of Cyprus, on a tour of Turkish communities and villages. This day we see the stark reality of the bitter, desperate, communal fighting that went on during the emergency. In one village we see where sixty homes were gutted. We see a whole community of Greek homes that had been dynamited and burned down. In one place where the Turks are resettling, people have been coming from miles around on Sundays to work on the new houses. But it is slow going and funds are low.

"It would be hard to exaggerate the fear and hate that exists between Greek and Turk here, not to mention the growing political divisions among the Greeks themselves. A river of bitterness runs very deep through this otherwise idyllic island. There's slanderous opposition to Makarios now, really vicious attacks, although he's still supported by a majority of the island.

"We join up with Dr. Kuchuk as he meets inside a cleaned-up barn with the heads of a village. It is really something that we have been brought here. First Dr. K. speaks, then Mr. Denktash. Then the villagers begin telling the two men about their problems and complaints. One old fellow, with a dark, lined face, points to a picture on the barn wall of a young man, his son. He was killed in the fighting. The old man wants a decent gravestone.

"At the next village, Denktash asks us to sing after Dr. Kuchuk has spoken. We sing a song in Turkish, which pays tribute to their island nation, and of the hope that together we can build a very different future. The people love the songs. We throw in some of our up-tempo country numbers like 'Freight Train Blues.' This meeting is held outside. At one point we all stop to shoo away a dog that keeps trying to bite someone's leg. It is a lively time.

"In Famagusta, the main port city, we meet with the mayor and union leaders who are members of the Communist Party and get a warm welcome.

"We are on English, Greek and Turkish radio and TV for nine days running, and the papers carry lots of articles. We give an impromptu performance for Rauf Denktash and his family in their home. [Denktash would succeed Dr. Kuchuk as leader of Turkish Cyprus and remain in that position into the twenty-first century.]

"The word we've been expecting about Africa comes through, and we receive it with mixed emotions. Three weeks ago we knew this island only as a very small dot on the map. But people here have taken us into their lives and shared their struggles and dreams with us, from a decent gravestone for a lost son, to hopes of peace for the generations to come. It's hard to describe how we've become so connected in such a short time, and we're disappointed that we'll miss the independence celebrations. But we're excited that Africa awaits. We take off via British European Airways to Ankara, Istanbul, Rome, Paris, and then to Liberia, Ghana, Nigeria, and God knows where."

"Vive le Congo!"

Steve, Paul and Ralph Colwell
(French translation by Charles Piguet and Eric Junod)

Au cœur de l'Afrique,
Pays magnifique,
Produit des merveilles de Dieu.
Rivières magiques,
Forêts des tropiques,
Peuples à l'esprit généreux.

Kivu, Katanga, Kasai, Leo,
Equateur, Orientale,
Que vive le Congo!

(In the heart of Africa
There's a magnificent country,
Overflowing with God's wonders.
With magical rivers and tropical forests
And people imbued with a generous spirit.)

10

RADIO CONGO AND
LES FRÈRES COLWELL

The call from the Congo came on May Day, 1960. "We were in Hokkaido, the northernmost tip of Japan, on the other side of the world," Ralph told a reporter who was interviewing the brothers in Milan. In the six months since their West Africa visit to Liberia, Nigeria, and Ghana, they'd participated in a year-end conference in Switzerland and worked in Western Europe and in the state of Kerala in southern India. In March, they arrived in Japan, where they toured for two months with members of the Seinendan youth organization.

In early 1960 the brothers visited Nigeria, Ghana, and Liberia, where their friend and associate John Amata (right), took them to meet villagers.

"It would have been hard for us to be any farther away from Africa," noted Steve. "We had about a day and a half to revel in the cool weather."

The Congo summons was no casual invitation. The situation there was desperate, they were told, and the clock was ticking. Tribal leaders attending the final Brussels conference on Congo independence had urgently requested help. The nation, home to some of the richest mineral deposits in the world, was in the birth pangs of impending self-rule after seventy-five years of Belgian control. In addition, the entire continent was a battlefield in the cold war. Delegates came to Caux after the Brussels conference and asked for an MRA "task force," including the Colwells, to tour the country presenting the film *Freedom*. The handover to sovereignty was set for June 30, just sixty days away.

Freedom, the first feature film made by Africans, had been dubbed into French, the lingua franca of the Congo. Originally written as a stage play, it dramatized the story of a country emerging into independence, complete with the arrogance of a colonial governor, the intrigues of politicians, and the challenges facing traditional leaders saddled with centuries of tribal animosity. The film ended with a surprising reconciliation, and an intriguing prototype for building a nation.

From Hong Kong to Calcutta, the Colwells flew on their first jet. "The Pan Am Boeing 707 was a fine ship," Ralph wrote, "but so new that even the cabin crew hadn't got used to it." In Delhi, they were received by the mayor, slept two nights on the roof of their host's home, and then had three days in Bombay for Paul to regain his strength. Their flight plan to Leopoldville, the Congo's capital, included a six-hour stopover at Nairobi in Kenya, then a plane change in Johannesburg, and then on to the Congo.

At the Leopoldville airport, the question was: where were their friends? All they knew was that their group was somewhere in the country, which was just about the size of Western Europe. Then they recalled hearing in India that showings of *Freedom* were to begin in Luluabourg. From the Pan Am office they called the Luluabourg mayor, who said he thought their friends were still in town.

Thirty days after the brothers landed in the Congo, a Belgian Air Force plane took off from Leopoldville to fly half of their international team on a two-week, 4,300 mile trip to the capital of every province in the country at the request of the governor general. There was no food served, so Steve made peanut butter, pickle, and mustard sandwiches for passengers and crew.

"All we could do," said Ralph, "was get on the next day's DC-4 for the three-hour flight to Luluabourg and hope for the best. As we approached the Luluabourg airstrip, we could see a small but modern and gracious provincial capital. Fortunately, our friend Bremer Hofmeyr was waiting for us on the tarmac. Our group here is extraordinary: John Amata is a graduate student leader from Nigeria, and Manasseh Moerane was vice president of the black teachers of South Africa; they wrote *Freedom* and have roles in the film. George Molefe and Bremer are from South Africa. Bremer's father-in-law was murdered during the Mau Mau insurgency. Leonard Kibuthu and Nahashon Ngare from Kenya were former Mau Mau fighters. Wilfred Hopcraft is a Kenya white settler. Eric Junod and Charles Piguet from Switzerland are skilled interpreters. From the USA there's Dr. Bill Close, who was chief resident surgeon at the Roosevelt Hospital in New York, Dave Beal and Tom Wilkes, whom we've worked with for years, and our little old selves."

In 1960, Ralph, Paul, and Steve were twenty-three, twenty-five, and twenty-seven years old. They didn't know it then, but they would be in the

Congo for an entire year, through independence, mutiny, military intervention, foreign manipulation, and chaos. Their letters home told the story.

Tribal conflict was tearing viciously at the fabric of African life. It had been happening for generations, and in some cases, centuries. A curfew was in place in Luluabourg because of the violence between the Luluas and the Balubas, the country's two main tribes. "Our greatest advocate here has been François Lwakabwanga, a Lulua who's been to Caux," Steve wrote. "He's greatly respected. He was bitterly anti-Baluba, and the Balubas cannot get over how his attitude toward them has changed. Lwakabwanga wrote a song with us in the local language, Chiluba, about the Balubas and Luluas coming together. After we sang it on the air the station was besieged with so many letters and calls the station manager decided to play it every day before and after the newscast."

Ralph: "One day we went out to Chief Kalemba's place. He is the Grand Chief of all the Luluas and had also visited Caux. We ran the film in his village square for a big crowd and ten neighboring chiefs. At a late dinner in his home, his secretary told us what happened a week earlier. *Freedom* was to be shown in a nearby town where there had been a massacre. A few kilometers from the village, just hours before the film was to begin, a truck carrying Balubas broke down in Lulua territory. Less than a month earlier, a truckload of Luluas had been murdered when their truck broke down in Baluba territory. But on that evening last week, because of the Chief's intervention, the Balubas were not hurt, and instead were helped on their way. At least forty-three lives were saved that day."

Belgium had agreed to give the country independence at short notice to avoid a repeat of the violent uprisings that Algeria and Kenya had seen. But the African population had not been educated and trained to take over. "No one knows, least of all the Congolese, what is going to happen here after June 30th," Ralph said.

Yet, something important would happen almost at once. It was radio. Steve wrote: "We've been meeting here in the capital with people who will run things after independence, and been invited to broadcast several programs. We've just taped three half-hour shows for Radio Leopoldville and two for Radio Brazzaville, one of the most powerful stations in the world. Brazzaville is just across the Congo River from Leo, and is the capital of the Republic of the

John Amata, Nigerian student leader and author and star of the all-African film, *Freedom*, speaks on Radio Congo. Swiss linguist Charles Piguet translates into French, the lingua franca of the country. More than 400 programs were broadcast in 1960 and '61. The Colwells sang at the beginning and end of all the shows, and eventually built a repertoire in five Congolese languages.

Congo, a French colony, which is to become independent on August 15. We sing at the beginning and end of all the programs. People from our group tell their personal experiences of conflict resolution, and everything is translated."

Radio in 1960 was the lifeblood and the nerve center of the country. As the sole means of communication, it played the combined roles of telephone, television, carrier pigeon, and jungle drum and gave millions their sense of identity as a nation. Every village, even in the remotest corners of the Congo, had at least one transistor radio.

Ralph: "Sometimes you feel you're on the tail of a comet. You just follow the leads and see where they take you. *Freedom* is often shown twice a day, and John Amata and Manasseh Moerane are meeting with key people non-stop. Next week they'll introduce the film in the most prominent white social club in the city, where no African has ever been allowed to enter as a guest. As I write this I'm sitting in a classroom of the new Lovanium University, and the film is on just down the corridor in the theater. This is an important place; so far in the whole of the Congo, there are just six university graduates, and only two medical doctors!"

Thirty days after the brothers landed in the Congo, a Belgian Air Force plane took off from Leopoldville to fly the international team to every province in the country at the request of the governor general. "Eight of us went and the other six stayed in the capital to meet with those coming for the celebrations as the 30th draws near," Ralph wrote. "We'll return to Leo on the 23rd, as far as we know now."

Two days later, on June 15, Steve described the reception at their first stop: "Coquilhatville (Mbandaka) sits right on the equator along the Congo River. It's the capitol of Equateur Province, carved out of the incredibly lush African rain forest. Enormous trees and plants tower above everything, their giant leaves dripping in the humidity. Nine hours after we landed the new Provincial Assembly saw *Freedom* in the Legislative Hall. The next morning we were received at the Assembly and besieged by members demanding a mass showing at the football stadium tonight." The welcome was similar in all the other provincial capitals of the country: Stanleyville (Kisangani), Bukavu, Elisabethville (Lumumbashi), Luluabourg (Kananga), and, on their return, Leopoldville (Kinshasha).

When the plane landed in Luluabourg, Ralph, and his instrument, got a jolt. "They were unloading the cargo when to my dismay I saw my bass dropping out of the hold! It landed right on its head, and its neck broke. That was not fun to watch. We took it into the city and somehow found an old Belgian wood-worker who bolted the neck back onto the body. For the rest of our time in the Congo, I played on a bolted bass, but I don't think anyone noticed."

Paul wrote brother Ted, who was turning fifteen, about the trip: "We just got back to Leo after a ten-day 4,300-mile trip to the six regional capitals of the country. We flew in a DC-3, the Belgian Air Force VIP plane. It was a terrific experience, but tiring work. No food was served on board so we had to buy our own supplies. Steve made us all peanut butter, pickle, and mustard sandwiches. Even the crew couldn't resist and were soon laying into them with us."

Irène Laure and her longtime colleague and interpreter, Denise Wood, arrived to support the group. "With Irène's background as a French resistance leader in World War II and a Socialist member of parliament, she is a power-ful addition," wrote Ralph. "On June 29 we were with her and Denise at the radio station taping a broadcast. Just before the program, who should walk in but cabinet member Albert Kalonji, who heads the Baluba tribe in the Kasai. He is strongly anti-Prime Minister Patrice Lumumba, and Balubas have been demonstrating against Lumumba's government. We'd been trying to see him for days. Kalonji breezed into the studio to make a radio appeal to his people. Mme. Laure engaged him in some serious conversation, and when he finished his broadcast we sang for him in Chiluba, his own language. He came for din-ner in our apartment."

Finally, the hour of Congo's independence arrived. In the Parliament on Thursday morning, June 30, the young King Baudouin of Belgium officially handed over the reins to the Congolese. The Colwells had been invited to per-form for fifteen minutes at the official banquet that evening.

"For the big event, we'd written a song with our Swiss colleagues called 'Vive le Congo!' that highlights the six original provinces," Ralph said. "When John Amata introduced us, people poured in from the side pavilions where they had

Transportation across flooded rivers in the Congo was often by innovative ferries of several dugout canoes strapped together. Passengers and crew pulled the craft across the river hand over hand via a stout rope.

been eating and stood around listening. There we were, in the middle of Africa, three Hollywood cowboys in our western garb singing in French and Lingala, 'Vive le Congo!' (Long Live the Congo!) and 'Mbote Batu Ya Congo' (Greetings, People of the Congo). During the festivities John was taken up to the head table and introduced to everyone there, from the Chief of State, President Kasavubu, on down to Prime Minister Lumumba, which isn't very far down. Lumumba said to John, '*Freedom* was magnificent. My heart is always open to you.' The wife of the Belgian cabinet minister in charge of Congolese Affairs had arranged for Lumumba and his cabinet to see the film the day before."

Steve wrote: "One morning President Joseph Kasavubu received all of us for forty minutes in his home where we performed for him and his family. He appears to be a man of integrity, quiet and soft-spoken. Lumumba is a different kettle of fish. He's fiery and charismatic with a bitterness, particularly against the Belgians, that is very evident and vocal. He is surrounded by people with radical agendas. But he seems open to us, so who knows? The new president of the Senate is Joseph Ileo, a highly respected leader who was probably the most instrumental person in bringing our group here. The first appointment he scheduled after his election was lunch at our apartment."

Ralph wrote: "I had an interesting birthday (July 2). Tom Wilkes and I went in the evening to a town outside Leo to show *Freedom*. We'd been invited by the mayor to present it as the climax of their independence celebrations. When we arrived there were thousands standing around a big bonfire, singing and dancing. We set up the screen on top of our Fiat van and the crowds all gathered around. It was a great audience, but half way through the show the mayor's secretary said we had to stop because of the curfew. However, after calling the police, we got permission to continue. We were told there had been serious disturbances in the neighboring community."

The disturbances were only beginning.

Paul (July 8): "We've just had quite a night and day, witnessing a revolt in this new country. By now you will have read about it. Even being on the spot we don't know exactly what is happening. Most of us are gathered in the apartment where Irène Laure is staying, on the 8th floor across from the Post Office. A couple of others are manning the phone at a different apartment to keep contact with the world. John Amata and the Kenyans, being Africans, are the only ones able to operate outside.

"Last night around midnight we were wakened by heavy traffic on the boulevard. We gave it little thought and went back to sleep. Then at 2:15 a.m. John Amata came crashing in to announce, 'The Army has burst out of the barracks and entered the city! Everyone is requested to go to the Regina Hotel immediately!' The hotel was a couple of blocks away, in the exact center of town. We dressed fast and raced over to the Regina, where a large crowd had gathered. When our whole group showed up, except for Steve and Ralph, who were in a private home, we decided to move to Irène's apartment. By this time people were leaving the Regina either for refuge in the Belgian Embassy or for the docks to find transportation to Brazzaville on the other side of the river. As far as we could make out there were no troops in the city at that point, only a mad rush of cars carrying women and children from the outlying suburbs to safety. The boats started evacuating at 3 a.m. and by 7 a.m. two thousand people had reached Brazzaville. Many more are on the other side by now, a large percentage of the twenty thousand Europeans living here in Leopoldville.

"The radio carried alarming reports and rumors of mass exodus, murder, and rape. Some of it may have been true, but up till now we understand that only one person has been injured. This doesn't detract from the gravity of the situation, however. Since daylight we have been watching small detachments of heavily armed troops tearing up and down the street in Jeeps and trucks.

It was not enough to get across the river. You had to get up the other side.

"Steve and Ralph out at their place didn't know about any of these events until their host barged into their bedroom at 7:30 a.m. They linked up with us later in the morning. Now the troops are generally out of hand, arresting people at random and obeying no one's orders. The situation approaches anarchy...Every solder is a law unto himself."

Ralph: "When the mutiny took place, we were living in six different places. About the time John Amata woke up those in the apartments, Eric Junod drove out near the military camp to a house where Tom Wilkes and Leonard Kibuthu were staying. Those three, coming back into town, were stopped by two soldiers just outside our apartment. One of them started coming at Eric with fixed bayonet. Eric dodged behind a big pillar, then dashed into the building slamming the door behind him. The soldier followed but didn't enter. Leonard, getting out of the car, then had quite a time calming down the soldier, who seemed slightly intoxicated but who luckily spoke Swahili, Leonard's own language.

"During the next three days we conceived a plan, and presented to the

Katanga soldiers marching through Elizabethville.

Minister of Information and Cultural Affairs, Mr. Kashamura, the idea of radio programs on a continuing basis. He had been under enormous pressure from people trying to intensify the conflict, and he responded enthusiastically to our proposition. On July 12 we made our first regular broadcast of fifteen minutes. It was put on the air twice daily, at the peak listening time just after the news at 8 p.m. and in the morning at 6:15 a.m.

"On Wednesday the 13th, John and some others were meeting with Senate President Joseph Ileo when Ileo got a call about trouble in La Cité, the African area of the capital. He said they better get back home because if the trouble spread they could be in danger. The night before two happily drunk unarmed soldiers had come into our apartment building and rung our bell, but we had all the lights out and didn't answer. The night before that, a soldier in the street fired at the building next to ours. Peering out a few minutes later we saw a Belgian flag hanging there. During those nights when soldiers were patrolling in Jeeps, those of us who were not Africans never showed our white faces over the railing of our balcony.

"By Wednesday afternoon, word had got around about the 'trouble,' and the streets were virtually empty. Solitary, branch-covered Jeeps passed by. Then, about 3 p.m., we saw them. Way down the street, trucks and Jeeps were advancing, coming from the center of town. We all ducked down. From behind the railing it slowly began to dawn on us that we were witnessing the re-entry of the Belgian military into Leopoldville. They made their way steadily up the divided boulevard, with heavy machine guns mounted fore and aft, and passed under us in quiet procession. The Congolese troops had disappeared.

On June 30, 1960, the Colwells performed at the official reception on Congo's Independence Day—three young Americans in Cowboy costumes singing in the heart of Africa.

"I admit to mixed emotions. Personally, I felt more secure, but what did this mean? Was there going to be open warfare? That would really be horrible. The Belgian convoy finally disappeared around the bend. A Congolese Jeep drove into the boulevard and then turned off again. For the next hour it seemed to us a kind of hide and seek between the armies. Way down the road in the center of town we could see a crowd gathered in the middle of the street. In the center we could just make out a Catholic priest with a scarlet sash around his middle. It was Bishop Joseph Malula. It turned out that he did heroic work in creating an entente between the two forces; the Belgian troops would stick to the European part of Leopoldville and the Congolese would stay in the African city. Driving to our broadcast that evening, we saw some Belgian and Congolese trucks stopped, and the soldiers seemed to be fraternizing. That night a convoy of 103 cars full of Belgian refugees going to the airport made its way down Boulevard Albert. When it reached the center of town we heard rifle and machine gun fire. Next day we learned that a group of mutinous soldiers had fired on the convoy and the Belgian Para-Commandos returned the fire. Three Congolese were killed.

"If the situation had been bad before, now it was ugly. Understandably, the Congolese deeply resented the return of the Belgian troops. We could feel that strongly at the radio station. It was a pretty unhappy atmosphere. But we kept at our shows, starting each one off with a little theme song in French we'd composed called 'Il Existe une Solution!' ('There Is an Answer!'). Radio Congo, however, began to broadcast anti-Belgian programs. From then until a few days ago there appeared to be an effort to incite the population, scare the daylights out of the Belgians, and generally create rancor and unrest. Night after night our program would come on sandwiched in between bitter commentary and a divisive slant to the news reports. Clearly the radio was the ideological hot spot in the nation, and there we were in the middle of it.

"Things came to a head again Friday the 15th. In Parliament that morning Lumumba had threatened to bring in the Russians, and we heard a wild rumor that he was calling on the Congolese Army to attack the Europeans that night. The Belgian Para-Commandos put barbed wire around our building and erected concrete barriers to use as firing positions. We packed our bags and were ready to go. I felt there was a good chance the attack was coming that day. I was plenty nervous. We waited all night in our darkened apartments unable to sleep. But the night passed without incident.

"At 6:30 Saturday morning we all got together to decide what to do. Some members of our group felt the wisest thing would be to evacuate, possibly to Brazzaville, and be ready to return if the situation stabilized. Others suggested

In Boma, in Katanga province, the travelers were honored to be invited to a wedding!

that the women and those with families plus ourselves, as we were the youngest, should go. That was not an option, as far as we were concerned. The more we talked about it, the more we realized that nothing would come of our mission if we didn't risk our own safety so we could stick by our Congolese friends who had invited us in the first place.

"The next day, Sunday, the first U.N. troops arrived, Tunisians, and they were cheered in the streets by the Congolese. Instantly the atmosphere began to lift. It was like the release of a safety valve to see them arrive. Next the Ghanaians and Moroccans came. The Ghanaian soldiers are great guys. They guard the radio now and have also been stationed outside our house since the Belgians withdrew (the last Belgian troops left the night of the 22nd). We've become friends with many of the Ghanaians. Most speak English or some kind of Pidgin English, so we can communicate all right. Since a few days now, it's the Swedish troops who have been guarding the main drag. They wear the blue U.N. helmets."

Every roadblock was temporary.

With few exceptions, Europeans had taken flight from Leopoldville, but the exceptions were noteworthy. "One morning at the height of the crisis," Steve said years later, "our colleague Dr. Bill Close left his apartment, crossed Boulevard Albert 1st, walked without security escort through the single line of European residences along the avenue, and entered La Cité. He went directly to the hospital where he volunteered his services as a physician. He and one elderly Belgian surgeon who had stayed were then the only doctors serving an African population of hundreds of thousands. He worked day in and day out around the clock, at times averaging an operation an hour. Close, a passionate and dedicated individual, was fluent in French. He had set aside a lucrative medical career. His wife and four children were back in Connecticut, expecting that he would be here for just a few weeks. In fact, he would be the only surgeon at the fifteen-hundred-bed Kinshasa General Hospital for an entire year, and spend sixteen years in the Congo, both as the chief doctor of the Army and as the personal physician to the president of the country."

Ralph wrote: "Last Monday at the radio station we ran into Mme. Blouin, a woman from Guinea in west Africa. She had been expelled from the Congo a few weeks before independence as an agitator. But she's back and has become a close friend and advisor to Vice-Premier Gizenga. We were in the studio when she walked in to do her broadcast. She recorded her program with four emotionless guardians standing by. The blow came on Wednesday night. We were sitting at home listening for our 8 p.m. broadcast (each show is put on tape the day before) when what should we hear but her announcing, "And now stay tuned for African Moral Re-Armament!" What followed was a half hour of Afro-pop, rumba, cha-cha-cha, and martial music, interspersed with highly charged, inflammatory commentary from Mme. Blouin. Our program only came on after.

"We had seen her buzzing around the station on Monday, and that's what she had been setting up. It was an apparent attempt on her part to confuse people about our work, create suspicions about our intentions as foreigners in the Congo, and get her own message across. The next day we arranged a meeting with the people in charge of the radio and discussed safeguarding the radio's integrity in this time of crisis. They were concerned about the various factions trying to use the radio for their own political advantage, which would result in dividing the country further. They face other challenges as well. Every European technician at the station has fled or quit; just two non-technicians remain. The Europeans trained very few Congolese in running a radio station, and there is really only one station in the whole country.

"The fact is that through the radio, what we're saying and singing has swept the capital. Several times a day people tell us, 'Everyone listens to your shows.' We hear it on the street, in offices, just all over town. A guy at the station told us today that he was at Lumumba's house the night before the P.M. left for New York. The P.M. was listening to our show and danced a little step to one of our songs. This same guy said, 'a neighbor rushes over to my house every morning to catch the early program at 6:15.'

"We're busy recording six songs for the Congo, and a local company has already agreed to make and sell the records here. We have four Congolese language songs, one French song for the Congo, and another number in French with a pretty hot banjo arrangement. A really popular one is 'Manioko mabe, fufu nayango m'pe mabe,' which says, 'You can't make good fufu out of bad manioc.' That's a song we worked on with Tabu Ley Rochereau (a popular bandleader who eventually would be a household name throughout Africa as a pioneer of the Soukous style of music). With Joseph Kabasele, who became an Afro-pop star, we wrote a song for the army, an important symbol of national unity. (Thirty-five years later, Rochereau, on tour in the U.S., was astounded to learn that Paul and Ralph were in the audience of his show in Tucson. He called them on stage, and told the crowd stories of the exploits of "these three white guys," in Africa. One member of his band remembered that as a kid he had sat on Ralph's lap after the brothers had played for his school.)

"Latest news: The radio is translating all the spoken word on our shows into the four main languages of the Congo: Lingala, Kikongo, Chiluba, and Swahili, for nationwide transmission. That's about it for now. We're all holding up. We've cleaned out every store in town of its stock of peanut butter, so we're in good health."

Paul turned a year older on August 6. A week later, he wrote his parents: "Thanks for the swift action on the shirts. We've worn most of the others right down to a frizzle, literally. Nudie did us proud again. Luckily our sizes haven't changed for the last ten years. Many thanks for your cable on my birthday, and thanks for your letter, Ma. In response to question No. 362, no, I didn't have a cake. We had hamburgers at my party, and boy, was the event a hit with the guys from the radio. The newscaster said afterwards, 'You all are the first white people who have shown themselves to us Congolese as just human beings like we are.' They really felt at home. Each had about six hamburgers, I think. At the end of the party Franco, the country's top recording artist, came in to pay his respects; Franco and his band, O.K. Jazz, is really famous here." (In the decades to come, Franco's unique guitar style would be emulated by musicians across the continent and the world, and become the modern guitar sound of Africa.)

Ralph (dated September 24): "What's happened just now must be shaking all of Africa. The bombshell exploded the night President Kasavubu went on the radio and dismissed Lumumba and some of his ministers. I could hardly believe my ears. Up to that point we had been living with growing concern as the government became more and more dictatorial, increasingly suppressing freedom, with Soviet technicians flooding in. You saw them everywhere. One day Steve and I were over at the office of the director of the radio. We were entering the door when a bus rolled up and four Russians got out. We got in just ahead of them, and waited with them to see the director. There may have been a bit of mutual uneasiness, but the atmosphere remained cordial. That day we heard that four of the best-trained technicians of the radio, good friends of ours, were being shipped off to study in Moscow and Guinea, which is the only country in Africa that has thrown in its lot with the

Eastern Bloc. That's not to say the others are pro-Western. It seems that Lumumba, not having got the response he was seeking from western countries, has decided turn to the 'East,' as Guinea has.

"President Kasavubu's broadcast came on a Monday night. Earlier that evening we were singing for about two hundred Ghanaian soldiers in an outdoor movie house. One minute before the film was to begin, an officer came running in saying that the troops had to get back to their camps immediately. Something big was happening. We went home wondering. Then at around 11 p.m. we got a call with the news. Many people had said President Kasavubu, a reserved and soft-spoken man, didn't have it in him to confront Lumumba. When the U.N. eventually came in to stabilize the situation, they closed down the radio and all the airports. The radio had become a divisive propaganda tool, and Kasavubu took exception to the airports being used for military operations, using Russian planes.

"Then a Ghanaian cabinet minister who came here on what was thought to be a 'good will mission' began sending reports unfavorable to Kasavubu back to Ghana's president Kwame Nkrumah. A few days later Ghana threatened to pull her troops out of the U.N. if the radio and airports weren't given back to the Congolese. The question was, of course, which Congolese?

"Now there was a severe political vacuum that the great powers rushed to fill. Both sides began to play hardball. Our group was independent and nonsectarian with no ties to any government agency. We were, perhaps naively, resolved to do our best to foster political and national harmony through peaceful means. Our efforts certainly supported the idea of creating an enlightened democratic system. But some agencies of the superpowers employed other means to achieve their goals. The results would play out in the weeks and months to come.

"During the time the radio was closed we'd become good friends with the Ghanaian colonel in charge of the troops guarding the facility. At 10 p.m. one night he was about to go to bed when he had a strong sense that he should go and inspect the station. His soldiers were already asleep, but the thought persisted so he roused an officer and they drove over to the radio. When they got there they discovered there were poor defenses for the soldiers in case of trouble, and that the back entrance was literally open to any intruder. During the night his troops dug trenches and put up barbed wire all around the station. Next day Lumumba arrived with two truckloads of armed Congolese soldiers demanding to get into the station to broadcast. 'Okay,' said our friend the Colonel, 'but I've got orders to let no one enter the station, and if you try to go in, my troops will fire.' After some very tense moments Lumumba and his men drove away. Lumumba is still sitting in the Prime Minister's residence, now protected by Sudanese soldiers. Two of his ministers were arrested today, and Mme. Blouin, whom we'd encountered at the radio station, is being expelled along with Lumumba's press secretary, who is French."

On a visit to Africa in 1963 Ralph shared birthday celebrations with the King of Burundi, who signed a photograph for the brothers. Later Ralph learned that the King and many of his family and friends had been murdered.

Then came the coup. The military, led by an unknown young colonel in the Congolese army, Joseph Mobutu, dismissed the government and took over the country. The news reached the world that night through a remarkable series of events.

Ralph: "At midnight on the night Colonel Mobutu declared that the military was taking control, Tom and I got a call from a British lieutenant in the Ghanaian army. I had been telling him quite casually that very day that I knew a fishing village along the Congo River where you could hire dugout canoes with outboard motors. The lieutenant told us over the phone that he had a pack of journalists who desperately needed to get the big news out to the world, but that the phone and telex systems were completely closed down for the night. There were no boats to be found to take them over to Brazzaville to dispatch their stories. Well, we had been to this little village on a sand bank along the river about four months ago, and had met a man with a boat.

"Dubious of our prospect for success, we agreed to drive the journalists out to see if we could find the village and get a boat across. We left at 12:30 a.m. We were far from optimistic; our visit to this tiny place four months back now seemed a very long time ago; it was a pitch black night, and under the jungle canopy along the river, blacker than black. To our own amazement, we eventually found the right little dirt road through the right part of the forest that led us to the right sand bar and the right little village. As we drove up cautiously with our headlights dimmed, we could see a single person sitting there, bending over a little fire to keep warm in the nighttime chill. Tom and I, the journalists, and our lieutenant friend quietly piled out of our cars.

"The village was asleep except for this one man. His role was to be watchman, and our unexpected arrival filled him with apprehension. At first he told us that it was impossible for anyone to go across the river at night. This was understandable, as the Congo is an enormous waterway that drains most of the country and much of Central Africa. But when a Canadian journalist pulled some money out of his pocket and waved it, the man seemed to change his mind. Soon he disappeared into the darkness to look for boatmen. He came back fifteen minutes later and led us past the fishermen's huts down to the river's edge, urging us to keep quiet and not to wake anyone; village people naturally don't like strangers prowling around at night, and we certainly fit that category. Before long some boatmen appeared. After a little hesitation the journalists climbed into a long dugout canoe and allowed themselves to be paddled silently out into the strong Congo current. They were soon out of sight. From that village it was a downstream trip to Brazzaville, so they probably arrived on the other side in twenty to thirty minutes. That's how the story got out to the world."

Steve (dated October 10): "Did you hear the latest sporting news? The Mutanda Meteors edged the Ghana 2nd Battalion team 36-28 in a basketball game last week. Paul Colwell was high scorer for the Meteors with 16 points! The Meteors, consisting of three Colwells, Dave Beal, and Tom Wilkes, have tentatively accepted to play the Ghana 1st Battalion Five next week. The 1st Battalion are the Ghana champs, so it ought to be a tight contest. (P.S. October 14: We lost to the 1st Battalion; they kicked our butts.)"

In late October, a calamitous reversal hit the Ghanaian soldiers. Their own government was removing them. Politics and ideology had trumped the goodwill the troops had created during their service in the Congo. After a deadly gun battle at the Ghanaian Embassy between Tunisian U.N. forces and the Congo Army, the Ghanaian ambassador was expelled and the embassy closed, another casualty of the cold war.

Paul: "Yesterday afternoon Colonel Atta, Commander of the Sudanese troops, gave a farewell celebration for the officers of the Ghana Second Battalion. The program ended with three Sudanese singing our song, 'Vive le Congo!'"

Paul (dated November 7): "You'll be glad to know that at the request of the Minister of Information we are back on the air again twice a day, morning and evening, from Monday through Friday. As you can imagine, that keeps us pretty busy. We sing two songs on each show as well as the theme song of the program. We now have eight full-fledged Congolese songs in five languages to draw on. We've learned that in remote areas of the country, our programs are broadcast over loudspeakers in village squares.

"Louis Armstrong gives a jazz concert here on Friday. We're invited to the official reception for Satchmo Friday morning."

Ralph wrote on January 16: "Happy New Year to all of you over there. For us the Christmas season started on the 24th morning when we visited the hospital where Dr. Bill Close works. We sang in four different places starting in the ward where the soldiers are. One soldier Bill takes care of had his jaw shot away in the fighting around the Ghana Embassy. We'd learned words in Lingala to the cowboy Christmas carol, 'There'll be a New World Beginning from Tonight.' In one ward there was a young guy lying just behind us. I looked back at one point and saw him wriggling around in bed in time with the music. The Catholic nurse gasped and said, 'He's moving his legs and arms!' He was supposed to be paralyzed from the neck down. I guess that was either a miracle or a vivid demonstration of just how much he loves music."

While the Colwells and their friends were buoyed by reports of the positive impact their work was having, horrendous divisions menaced the new country. A U.S. National Intelligence Estimate called the situation "political instability on a grand scale." The government in Leopoldville controlled just two of the Congo's six provinces. A competing Soviet-backed government based in Stanleyville and loyal to former Prime Minister Lumumba controlled two other provinces. The diamond-rich province of South Kasai had recently seceded and was functioning as a separate state, and the copper-rich Katanga province had stoutly declared its sovereignty a fortnight after Congo independence. On December 1, troops loyal to Colonel Mobutu arrested Patrice Lumumba in the city of Port Francqui.

Ralph (January 16): "At 8 a.m. tomorrow we take off by road for a major tour of Katanga. The first city will be Elisabethville, where Lumumba is being held. I expect we'll be moving at a pretty fast pace in the months ahead."

It was the rainy season, and swollen rivers would interrupt the pace more than once. Innovative local ferries provided passage. Floatation was via six or seven large dugout canoes strapped side-by-side, supporting a decking of heavy planks. Propulsion was via a stout rope stretched tightly across the river. As a single vehicle (the ferry's capacity) was ever so carefully driven down the slippery bank and inched onto the deck, the crew pulled hard on the rope to keep the ferry in contact with the shore, their muscles the only deterrent against disaster. Once the vehicle was safely aboard, crew and passengers turned about, grasped the rope, and pulled the ferry to the other side. Getting the vehicle up the muddy bank from the landing frequently required all hands to push.

The convoy consisted of a Volkswagen Kombi minibus, a two-door Volkswagen bug, and a Ford pickup with a shell cover. During seven adventurous weeks in Katanga, the international group visited the principal tribal centers and cities. They received a memorable response. In Musumba on February 8, the drummers of Mwami Mwata-Yamvo, grand chief of the Lunda and traditional ruler of Katanga, sounded a beat heard for fifteen kilometers to summon people to the palace to honor the visitors.

On a second visit to Elisabethville, after the Colwells sang for the grand chief of all the Balubas in Katanga, one of the chief's party presented a thousand franc note to each brother.

"How about that?" Steve reflected later. "Financial aid from the Congo to America! It was a welcome gift to those of us working with no salary."

The Colwells' singing in the chief's own language, according to a press report, "created a sensation." The provincial minister of justice arranged to record the songs.

Only when they returned to Leopoldville did the travelers learn that on January 17, the day they had set out for Elisabethville, Patrice Lumumba had been shot by a firing squad at a remote site near that same city.

After a few days in the capital for instrumental and physical "retuning," the group headed for the Bas Congo, or Lower Congo, where they planned to present *Freedom* at tribal centers and military bases, and for Indonesian U.N. forces occupying the important Kitona Air Base at the mouth of the Congo River. The Colwells made the trip in an ancient Ford Tri-Motor airplane. The Asian battalion, soon to leave the Congo after eight months service, cheered wildly when the brothers sang to them in Indonesian. At another base, armed soldiers, suspicious of the nature of the event, patrolled the perimeter in case of a "U.N. trick," until the brothers sang for them in Lingala.

Years later, Dave Beal told a friend about his vivid memory of an outdoor showing of *Freedom* in the port city of Matadi, a hundred miles downriver from Leopoldville. "There was a big crowd overflowing the soccer field, I don't know how many thousands, and because of the numbers we had placed the projector in the middle of the field on a couple of sturdy tables, stacked one on top of the other. We'd heard there had been some police activity in the village earlier, but apparently it hadn't kept anyone away. The Colwells sang first, and then we started the film. It all went well until very near the end when there was some kind of disturbance on the edge of the crowd. I never did find out what it was, but it was instantly obvious that people wanted to avoid provoking the police, who were always quick to overreact. In what seemed like thirty seconds, everyone was gone. It was a human stampede. Ralph was grabbing a nap in a VW bug

"Boma, a town at the mouth of the Congo River was the hometown of our guide, translator, and co-songwriter Henri Konde, who spent several months with us during our Congo sojourn. Henri wrote the Lingala and Kikongo lyrics to several of our African songs. He invited us to stay with his family. When we left our van was stuffed with our equipment and a goat that the Konde family generously presented to us. The goat was christened with the French name 'Donc.'"

parked in back of the crowd and woke up to the thunder of thousands of feet hurtling by as if they were drumming the ground—and then complete quiet. He stepped out of the car, and there on the field was a sea of sandals that had been left behind. People had literally run out of their shoes. They knocked over the tables, the projector went flying, and Tom Wilkes and I nearly got trampled. Fortunately, no one was hurt, and Tom and I were able to repair the bent parts of the projector that night in our hotel."

At the strategic port of Matadi, where fighting a month earlier between U.N. forces and the Congo Army had made world news, the Colwells found that heavy concentrations of soldiers and police had set up roadblocks to prevent the return of foreign troops.

Ralph: "The local militia suspected that we were U.N., who by this time were regarded as occupiers. At one roadblock they demanded that we get out of our minivan. We said, *'Nous sommes les Frères Colwell.'* Their faces lighted up but they weren't totally convinced. So we started singing 'Vive le Congo!' That did it. We were for real. We were offered palm wine and shook many hands. They led us into the village and said, 'Put on a show!' Of course we obliged. The village kids packed in around us so tightly we could hardly strum. But it was getting late in the day and we had to get to our next destination. So while our Swiss colleague Eric Junod engaged them in conversation, we edged back to our van, slipped inside, and then waited for Eric to jump in. We sped off, waving merrily to the villagers."

Paul: "From Matadi we drove down to Boma, a town at the mouth of the Congo River where Portuguese explorers first landed many centuries ago. This was the hometown of our guide, translator, and co-songwriter Henri Konde, who spent several months with us during our Congo sojourn. Henri wrote the Lingala and Kikongo lyrics to several of our African songs. He invited us to stay with his family. This was the first time we had been able to live in an African home—mud walls, thatched roof, and as warm and welcoming as any place we had ever been. And the food, fufu topped with peanut sauce and spiced with pili-pili, was the hottest we'd tasted since south India. When we left for Leopoldville several days later, our Fiat van was stuffed with our equipment and a goat that the Konde family generously presented to us. The goat was christened with the French name 'Donc.'"

Steve (June 23): "We've come full circle. We arrived here in Luluabourg the day before yesterday via a U.N. plane. This was the first place we came to in the Congo a year ago, and it was almost like coming home. But not quite. Now the grasses and shrubbery are overgrown. Most of the shops are closed, and the few that are open have little merchandise. We've had to scrounge to find anything to eat. Soup and toast are our staples, with a little jam if we're lucky.

"Do you remember us writing about Francois Lwakabwanga? He is now chief of cabinet for the president of North Kasai. When the trouble hit Luluabourg a few weeks ago the Army massacred more than a hundred people. All the cabinet ministers disappeared. Francois was one of the few officials who stayed and fought to restore order. He arranged for the president and his family to see *Freedom* in his home last night."

During 1960 and 1961, the Colwell brothers and their friends made more than four hundred broadcasts over Radio Congo in the four indigenous languages and in French. Monsignor Joseph Malula, the auxiliary bishop of Leopoldville, described the programs as "a voice of sanity to the nation."

Turmoil continued in the Congo. The brothers returned briefly in 1962. The song they wrote for the nation's independence had become an enduring hit; "Vive le Congo!" was loved and sung by millions. The Colwells were told that their song continued to be played as the signature tune for the national radio newscasts long after they left the country. In 1964, the country's name was changed to the Democratic Republic of the Congo, and to Zaire in 1971, then back to the Democratic Republic of Congo at the end of the century.

In 1968, Ralph and his new bride, Debbie, accompanied an Up with People cast that celebrated eight years of Congo independence, performing in Kinshasa and Lubumbashi. Mobutu Sese Seko's rule of the country would last until his overthrow in 1997. Since then, nearly four million Congolese have died in civil wars, mostly of disease and starvation.

Paul comments: "The Congo is always on our hearts. It is very telling that this unimaginable human tragedy has played out while the wealthy nations essentially have stood by and focused on other priorities more directly impacting their economic and security interests. I suggest that this issue should be pushed up on the priority list. And perhaps one day, the lives of those who have the least will be valued as much as those who have the most."

Reflecting on their African experience, Ralph said, "We witnessed the beginning of the end of the European colonial era. But there were thousands of nongovernment people who came to Africa and served selflessly to bring modern education and health care. Many are still there. It's easy to feel that our efforts have been in vain, swept away by the hurricane of history. In retrospect, the issues during that time may seem less complex and overwhelming than they are today. But I believe small, seemingly insignificant victories, like rays of light, can illuminate the future. One night in 1960 during a showing of *Freedom*, I sat down on the floor

One more river.

of a packed hall with a crowd of Congolese kids and their families who were watching the movie, one white face in a sea of black. Leonard Kibuthu, the former Mau Mau fighter, sat down next to me and said, 'I never thought this could be possible—white and black together, everyone equal.'"

"With Everything Changing"

Paul Colwell and Bill Cates

There stood an old man,
Tears filling his eyes,
They were tearing the courthouse down,
And he was saying goodbye.

With everything changing,
Does anything stay the same,
A hope you can cling to,
Someone who needs you,
A love that can lead you everyday?

Go talk to the old man,
Help him understand.
Walk by the young man's side
And lend him a hand.

With everything changing,
Does anything stay the same,
A hope you can cling to,
Someone who needs you,
A love that can lead you everyday?

11

OUT OF AFRICA

Leaving a continent was by now not a new experience for the Colwell brothers. They had done it numerous times, and while leaving always produced a poignant blip on the radar of their emotions, some new challenge usually lay ahead. This time, however, there was a difference. Ralph's first inkling of it came at the end of the long flight from the Congo in 1961. It was a picture-perfect June day, and as the big Sabena Airlines jet banked smoothly for its approach to the airport, the landscape below was like a patchwork in the colors of spring.

"We were landing at Brussels when I looked out the window at that peaceful, ordered countryside, and was suddenly aware of a huge letdown. 'This is the end of a pivotal chapter of our lives,' I thought. 'Nothing can ever top it.'"

The feeling of a phase ending was reinforced sixty days later with the death of Frank Buchman at Freudenstadt in Germany. With Herb Allen, they traveled from Caux to Freudenstadt to join the throngs attending Buchman's memorial service.

At the end of the year, the brothers flew to Brazil for a Latin American conference. They sang on the docks of Rio de Janeiro as a backup group for cowboy star Roy Rogers as thousands of dockworkers swarmed around them.

"I remember a restless feeling then about where we were heading," Ralph said. What he was feeling was considerably more than restlessness: one evening

The brothers played on the docks of Rio de Janeiro in 1961 as a backup group for country western star Roy Rogers, and gave their own concert for thousands of Brazilians who flocked to hear them. They would soon play in a big show at the huge new 200,000-seat Maracanã soccer stadium. But they were beginning to wonder where they were heading with their music, and their lives.

he'd called Varig Airlines to inquire about a ticket to California. His brothers didn't know about that until decades later.

"We kept our focus," Steve said, "because there was always a crucial situation to consider, key national figure to sing for, world hotspot to travel to, or the next big event to prepare for that challenged us. In Rio, for instance, we had a show coming up in the huge 200,000-seat Maracanã soccer stadium. Also, once a performer, always one; you never got tired of the applause. But having said that, the feeling of accomplishment, of a show well performed and a sense that we were reaching people, was often tempered by sharp admonishments from some of the leadership to do better and live more dedicated lives. My lifelong stuttering problem was exacerbated by the stress I felt. (Maybe that's why I started turning gray in my twenties?) Anyway, we seemed to be playing more and more of an adjunct role. Of course, at conferences, we pitched in like everybody else because we were committed, but in the early sixties, our focus definitely became diffused."

Loyal to a fault, the brothers rarely articulated this. "I guess you could say it started as questioning," Paul said, "then it became concern, and eventually frustration. The world wasn't all black and white; it was Technicolor. There was some dimension of relevance we hadn't discovered yet."

Ralph was more specific: "I think some people we worked with took for granted we would always be reliable foot soldiers, but that seemed like a suffocating blanket of control. We needed to grow as musicians and as people."

The stamps in the passports of the Colwells and Allen kept on coming during the next three years: Allen in a dozen countries from Finland and Ireland to Japan and Korea, with Olympic gold medalists John Sayre and Rusty Wailes performing in the musical review *Space Is So Startling*. Allen cowrote the music and was music director of the show.

"Herb was tireless," recalled Ted Colwell, who was in the cast. "We toured for six months in India, helping Rajmohan Ghandi generate mass rallies for a 'clean, strong, and united India.' One rally on the beach at Mumbai drew seventy thousand people. Herb arranged the show's music for large orchestras. I remember him working into the nights, scoring charts by hand for all the instruments."

The Colwells spent a solid year up and down the boot of Italy with friend and gifted lyricist Paulo Marchetti; recorded six records on the Durium label as "I Fratellli Colwell"; and performed in hundreds of venues in support of the stage production *El Condor,* created by students from across Latin America. "They wrote a new song for every city we visited," said Jerry von Teuber, who traveled with them, "and the mayor, chief of police, and the head of the local mafia were always in the front row."

They were in Europe with Chinese youth and their theatrical play *The Dragon;* with Japanese youth and *The Tiger;* in Cairo with the head of the Arab League; in Khartoum, Sudan, with El Mahdi in his palace; in Cape Town and the Congo with German coal miners and their dramatic play *Hoffnung* (Hope); in Zimbabwe with blacks and whites; and in Burundi with the king.

Kirsten Andersen (Larsen) from Denmark, then an executive secretary who was traveling with the group during the 1962 African tour, retained a vivid memory of the visit. "One night in the Congo, which for some reason I can't now explain, I was driving alone to the Leopoldville airport in Eric Junod's Opel Kapitan to pick up people arriving to join our group. Suddenly, three armed soldiers flagged me down. They stuck their heads and guns into the car and began opening the doors. They were giving commands but I couldn't understand anything; I didn't know if I was to get out or if they were getting in. I was terrified, just as frightened as when I was fifteen and on a streetcar in Copenhagen, and Gestapo troopers boarded looking for members of the resistance. I had copies of the underground newspaper wrapped around me beneath my clothes, and only got away by throwing a tantrum. That night in the Congo, although I didn't speak French, I was somehow able to come out with, *'Je suis avec Les Frères Colwell!' (I'm with the Colwell Brothers!)* It had been two years since the brothers made those radio broadcasts, but I was immediately waved ahead."

The Colwells flew to London at the end of April 1964 and conferred with friends about how to update their presentation and become reacquainted with the popular music scene of the West. "It's time to modernize," George Fraser advised. Within days, they were proud owners of their first electric instruments. Active weeks of rehearsal and performance followed, including a visit to the Cavern Club in Liverpool of Beatles fame.

For more than a decade, the brothers had sung and played almost everywhere but home. In June that would change, in what would become the third hinge point of their lives.

"Up with People"

Paul and Ralph Colwell

Well, it happened just this morning,
As I was walking down the street,
A milkman and a postman
And policeman I did meet.
There in every window
And in every single door
I recognized people
I'd never noticed before.

Up, up with people,
You meet 'em wherever you go.
Up, up with people,
They're the best kind of folks we know.
If more people were for people,
All people everywhere,
There'd be a lot less people
To worry about
And a lot more people who care.

12

UP WITH PEOPLE:
BIRTH OF A PHENOMENON

When the Colwells and Allen steamed into the Mackinac Island harbor in 1964 to take part in the student leadership conference, they had no great expectations for the event. There hadn't been headlines about it, or even a mention on an inside page somewhere. What was happening on the island was obviously under the media radar screen. But the gathering would be significant for the globetrotting musicians, and ultimately have an international impact.

Pace, a new *Life*-sized youth oriented magazine, would feature the conference in its premier issue that fall and bravely attempt to describe what happened there:

A new national magazine gave the first glimpse of the electric atmosphere of the Great Lakes conference in 1964. The phenomenon of Up with People started here, but it was just beginning.

The Moral Re-Armament Conference buildings on Mackinac Island, Michigan.

CALIFORNIA DELEGATIO
CONFERENCE FOR
TOMORROW'S AMERIC
MACKINAC ISLAND, MICHIGAN

we started here

Take the excitement of a political convention, add to it the physical exertion of a basic training camp, the best of a hootenanny and the urgency of a Summit Conference, and you begin to get an idea of what took place on Mackinac Island at the Conference for Tomorrow's America this summer. 2,400 high school and college students from all across America and Canada as well as from Europe and Latin America took part.

A working gravel barge made to resemble a Mississippi River show-boat provided a floating stage from which the young performers gave their show to audiences around the Great Lakes.

British journalist Peter Howard gave the keynote address at the 1964 Mackinac conference. Conference chairman J. Blanton Belk (below) would become Up with People's founding president.

SHOWBOAT

"Take the excitement of a political convention, add to it the physical exertion of a basic training camp, the beat of a hootenanny and the urgency of a Summit Conference, and you begin to get an idea of what took place this summer on Mackinac Island at the Conference for Tomorrow's America. 2,400 high school and college students from all across America and Canada as well as from Europe and Latin America took part."

The dynamism of the event took the Colwells and Allen by surprise, which surprised a friend who had known them for years. Surely, their experiences had been without equal, in the last three years alone picking up pages of passport stamps from around the world. Yet this gathering was like nothing they'd ever seen. At the opening session of the conference, in a jam-packed auditorium built as a giant teepee, scores of Native Americans were introduced to the cheers of the crowd overflowing into the hallways, waving banners of their states and regions. Student body presidents were there, delegates from other countries, Olympic gold medalists, musicians with great talent, untalented people with energy and enthusiasm. The prime minister of Trinidad and Tobago sent the country's National Steel Band. Why had they all come?

They'd been pointed to the event the preceding winter when Peter Howard addressed student gatherings at universities across the United States. Howard had been one of Britain's foremost political columnists, and dynamically spoke to the concerns of the generation. He had headed Moral Re-Armament since Frank Buchman died in 1961, and was convinced that the key to a just society was in the eager, if untested, hands of the young. And here they were, idealism and energy unleashed, thousands intent on contributing to society, on "changing the world," as they put it.

"There's no question," Ralph said, "that I arrived back on my native soil with some anti-American bias that had seeped in through years of viewing the U.S. through other people's eyes. So, it was quite a shock to walk into that huge hall and feel the dynamism of those young delegates. It was very much the energy of sixties youth who were

In 1965 the cast of *Sing Out '65* gave performances for American troops stationed at Korea's DMZ, the no man's land between North and South Korea. The *Sing Out* show was the predecessor of *Up with People,* which would become the second longest-running musical of the 20th century.

embracing idealism, rebellion, and revolution. In the 1930s, Dr. Buchman had spoken of a movement to remake the world. That jargon was beginning to make its way into the mainstream, and by 1964, with the power of the civil rights movement, the war in Vietnam, and the threat of a cold war bursting into flames, it wasn't crazy to talk about changing the world. And at that conference, we were smacked in the face with the energy, excitement, and idealism of the astounding array of young people in attendance. Almost immediately, my ideas and feelings about the U.S. began to shift."

Paul too was seeking a different focus. "We were not the same trio when we returned to the U.S. in 1964 as when we left in '53. We'd dropped out of the mainstream then, and for a decade had worked pretty much in the developing world. Our globe-spanning gig was an unusual training ground, and perhaps an unlikely one, but through it, we'd gained a consciousness of the whole human race. The question we were asking ourselves now was, where do we go from here?

"We had just acquired electric instruments in London. In our travels before that time, we were country/folk artists playing acoustic instruments, with Ralph on the standup bass. I played electric guitar on rare occasions, but rock 'n' roll changed all that. Even Bob Dylan went electric. We practiced intensely on our new instruments and began writing songs for a different market."

Erected at the start of the conference, a big top tent towered above the athletic field along the Straits of Mackinac. Hootenannies happened there most evenings, in entertaining contrast to the serious, far-ranging deliberations of the day. In a natural segue from their decade of performing and coaching others, the Colwells and Allen became silver threads in the big tent events, helping young musicians uncork their creativity and put together loosely linked productions, each with a charm of its own.

"We had no idea what the shows might lead to, but we knew that our roles were to help the performers express their convictions through music," Herb said. "What Color is God's Skin?" written by Tom Wilkes and Canadian David Stevenson, pierced the very heart of prejudice. A phenomenal nineteen-year-old drummer named Bob Quesnel brought down the house every night.

At a planning session during one of the periodic summer storms that churned the Great Lakes into scary seas and had shut down the big top for the evening, conference chairman Blanton Belk voiced a suggestion that caught the imagination of everyone. Why not create a showboat that could sail to Great Lakes harbors so you could perform for people in all those communities?

Well, why not? A motorized gravel barge was turned into a riverboat replica that powered as a floating stage into marinas around the lake.

That fall, teams from the Mackinac conference fanned out across the continent to promote Peter Howard's latest book, *Design for Dedication*, and build a groundswell for the following year's conference. "When we'd arrived back in the States," Steve recalled, "our ever-generous parents had given us a welcome-home gift of a Pontiac station wagon. It was something of a culture shock to see the wide streets in cities, with cars traveling at moderate speeds, staying in lanes, and actually stopping at stop signs. In some places we'd worked, streets were narrow and congested, drivers leaned on their horns, and the mix of vehicles, from buses to bicycles to ox carts, made travel hair-raising. Add in driving on the left side of the road in small economy cars with barely room for the three of us and our instruments, especially Ralph's bass, and you get the picture."

"In September, after playing the Santa Fe County Fair with Herb and the Navajo Tribal Fair in Window Rock, Arizona," Ralph said, "we went on the road with our longtime friend and now writer/manager, David Allen, and our drummer, Bob Quesnel, to create a new sound and new songs that could hold their own in the rockin' sixties."

They headed to West Virginia, and within a week the energetic Quesnel, with a keen sense of what would promote the *Sing Out* program, announced, "I'm going to get into the Guinness Book of World Records for nonstop drumming!" It was also an Olympic year and he called it his own Olympic event. The run at the record quickly became hot news in the coal mining towns of southern West Virginia. "The local and national press covered it. One night while Bob was drumming away, CBS news called to interview him.

On a national show on the NBC television network, Herb Allen, here in silhouette, conducted the cast.

"When they asked, 'Why are you doing this?' Bob replied, 'Someone has to stay awake while the nation sleeps.' Carefully following Guinness's exacting rules, Quesnel played and played, for crowds in school gymnasiums, on a flatbed truck riding down Main Street, traveling from town to town, while he was eating, using the restroom, and showering. High school cheerleaders cheered him on."

And the Colwells kept him awake. "We practically had to prop him up at times," Paul said, "and prop ourselves up too. But he broke the old record of one hundred hours and two minutes, by drumming for one hundred hours and twenty minutes. The mayor of Welch, West Virginia made a speech and an ambulance drove him away to the local clinic to make sure he was all right. Then he slept for fourteen hours."

In the spring, the brothers and David Allen joined Rusty Wailes on a whirlwind speaking tour of a dozen Southern campuses. At each university, the Colwells introduced Wailes' talk with a special song: for Duke, Bethune Cookman, Clemson, Florida, Florida State, Mississippi State College for Women, and more.

That same season, Herb Allen introduced steel band music to America with a cross-country tour of the National Steel Band of Trinidad and Tobago. Bandleader Cliff Alexis, who became a steel band legend and a teacher at Northern Illinois University, had vivid memories of the time. "I was twenty-seven years old, and the first night at the Mackinac conference opened my eyes to the world. After the tour, I went back to Trinidad, and then moved to the U.S. where I've lived now for forty years. I've kept in touch with Herb and the Colwells ever since."

Students at Jordan High School in Watts cheer the show. *Up with People* was the first event at the school after the Los Angeles race riots that claimed 34 lives.

When Peter Howard died of a sudden illness in February 1965, the leadership role of this fast-evolving, definition-defying youth initiative fell on the shoulders of his close associate Blanton Belk.

Paul: "In April 1965, Blanton convened a group of us at his home in Tucson, Arizona, along with a handful of student body presidents from universities around the country. I remember feeling as I drove into Tucscon that there were exciting developments on the horizon. The purpose of the meeting was to brainstorm and plan the upcoming 'Modernizing America' conference at Mackinac Island. During the discussion my brothers and I proposed that we put together a weekly musical 'happening' at the conference as a showcase for talent and creative expression. It would be in an informal, spontaneous coffee-house format.

"However, by the time we premiered it early in July, it had grown into a full-blown variety show with lights, costumes, a stage band, and original and international dances and songs with Herb Allen conducting and we three brothers hosting and performing. The response to our first 'show' was unanimous—we should take it on the road! By the second week, the cast had expanded to over one hundred performers. We launched the song, 'Up with People!' that we had just finished that week.

"There were distinguished guests in the audience from Washington and Tokyo. Invitations started coming in, and it was clear we had to quickly get this production ready for public consumption. Renowned West End director Henry Cass flew in from London with choreographer Bridget Espinosa to help turn our fledgling creation into a professional quality musical revue."

Ralph described the moment: "After we previewed our glorified talent show for Mr. Cass and Ms. Espinosa, we nervously gathered around them backstage to hear their reaction. Mr. Cass's career was steeped in Shakespeare and classical theater. Surely, he would be quite critical and even a bit condescending. To our astonishment, he said, 'I wouldn't touch it!' Of course, they did change and tighten things up. But on the whole, they left the spontaneous exuberance and energy intact."

At the beginning of August, with their newly named show, *Sing Out '65*, ready to debut, the troupe traveled to the East Coast. Following their "world premiere" in Stamford, Connecticut, they bused to Cape Cod where they acquired another barge and performed at Martha's Vineyard and storied Cape harbors. *Sing Out '65* was then featured at the World's Fair in New York City and later in the month played to a packed ballroom at the Washington, D.C., Hilton, sponsored by seventy-two members of the U.S. Congress. The cast members took a special train to California and were invited to perform for high school students in the Watts area of Los Angeles immediately after race riots that had resulted in more than thirty deaths that summer. Then they filled the Hollywood Bowl before taking off on a lightning trip to Japan. There, at the invitation of the prime minister, they performed in a packed sports arena with the prime minister in attendance, for students at Waseda University, and in the ancient Kabuki Theater where women had never before been allowed on stage. In South Korea, they played for American troops guarding the

Paul and Ralph composing, directing, thinking.

demilitarized zone and gave public shows in Seoul. Landing back in California, the company would soon see the birth of a mirror image show. Ted Colwell, now nineteen years old, played guitar in the headline group, along with Dan Broadhurst, David Allen and Fred Morgan. They were called "The Colwell Four." Their show was dubbed "Cast B." The company returning from Asia became "Cast A."

Cast B's premiere was also its dress rehearsal. Eric Millar, an accomplished jazz pianist but a neophyte maestro, wielded the baton—with help. "Eric was in the orchestra pit," said Herb Allen, "but in the first performance, so was I. I conducted him while he conducted the cast!"

Then came an avalanche of duplication. Satellite shows started popping up around the planet. Sing Outs had an instant and seemingly irresistible attraction to young people eager to participate in the mainstream of their time. Within twelve months of the "lift-off" in Cape Cod, one hundred-fifty regional Sing Outs had sprung up across the United States, and a hundred more across the world. *Sing Out '65* songs were being picked up everywhere, especially "Up with People." Before the end of the year the Colwells, Herb, and their cast had

On a summer evening in Paris, thousands gathered in the twilight to watch the show against a backdrop of one of France's historic monuments.

taped their first national TV special, which aired on CBS. Two more national TV specials would follow: one on NBC in 1967 and another on CBS in 1973. Writer David Allen recorded that during one week in September 1966 regional Sing Outs across America performed live before one hundred thousand people:

"Eventually there were four hundred local and regional shows worldwide with an estimated sixty thousand participants. In the U.S. in 1966, there were fourteen casts in California, four in Florida, three in Idaho, five in Kentucky and Ohio, two in Wyoming, and eleven in Tennessee. Overseas there were sixteen casts in various parts of Germany; *Harambee Africa* in Kenya and Uganda; *Springbok Stampede* in South Africa; *Sing-Out Korea* in Seoul; *Sing Out Finland* in Scandinavia; *India Arise* in India; and *Sing Out Venezuela, Sing Out Panama, Sing Out Jamaica*, and five casts of *Sing Out Puerto Rico* in Latin America. Down under, it was *Sing Out Australia*. In Tokyo, *Let's Go '66* was performing weekly on national television. This was the explosive beginning of Up with People."

It was the opening chapter in an extraordinary story. A third traveling company, "Cast C," was formed at Estes Park, Colorado, when Sing Out groups from across North America came together in 1966. In the summers of 1967 and '68, Sing Out people from around the world assembled at Fort Slocum, a former island military base in Long Island Sound, New York. The music of multiple traditions began echoing through the performances.

In 1967, Blanton Belk resigned his position as director of MRA in the United States, and in 1968 incorporated Up with People as a non-sectarian, educational and cultural organization with the mission of promoting understanding around the world. Belk was Up with People's president, CEO, and board chairman for twenty-five years and remained active in the organization after that.

"Herb is famous for telling puns," Paul said. "He takes them seriously. With Herb, jokes are no laughing matter."

In those years, the Colwells were typically the lead group of their cast, and in collaboration with others wrote many of the songs for the shows. Herb Allen was music director.

In the years that followed, at least five casts toured simultaneously. Cast members were given generous hospitality by tens of thousands of host families in thousands of cities large and small around the world. Each company toured outside the United States for several months. Sponsors ranged from small organizations such as the newspaper of a Midwestern town to multinational giants such as Sears, General Motors, Toyota, and Coca-Cola.

Mentions in the media occasionally approached hyperbole: "The organization resonates with the hopes and dreams of millions for a better world." The Colwells and Herb Allen never asserted anything like that, but

they felt the waves of support coming back from audiences, host families, and sponsoring organizations.

"For years, we'd given our all with Moral Re-Armament," Ralph said, "and now this was moving far beyond us. We had no forewarning of the impact Up with People was going to have. Of course, we're enormously gratified, and proud to have been part of launching such a global endeavor. And we do want to emphasize 'part.' We've been part of a team of very dedicated people. From the beginning, Blanton Belk and a talented global staff have guided the organization's growth and inspired students with an exciting vision of their potential."

Paul: "From the mid-'60s on, we spent a good portion of our waking hours (sleep was often in short supply) trying to come up with new music, new ideas, and new concepts. Our show, like the overall Up with People program, was evolving throughout those first five years, as new songs were added and old ones dropped. In 1971, the duration of student participation changed from an open-ended one to a one-year enrollment. That year also marked the beginning of writing a brand-new show every two years."

Ralph said: "As Up with People grew, we began to realize that we had to start planning

Lynne Morris with the cast, and the bullring at Madrid, Spain.

for the futures of all those who were participating as management and staff of our new enterprise. From 1965 to 1970, we operated on the MRA model of volunteering our time and talents with no direct remuneration. In fact, my brothers and I and Herb, along with the hundreds of other full-time MRA staff members, had never received a penny of pay for our efforts. We depended almost entirely on the generosity and hospitality of hundreds, probably thousands, of supporters all over the world for food and board and the costs of traveling. But in 1970, Blanton Belk and the senior management realized that we were in this for the long haul. Many of us were starting families, renting apartments, buying homes and were becoming taxable members of society. I can remember my elation when I received my first paycheck in 1970. We had just rented a nice two-bedroom apartment overlooking the Pacific Ocean in San Clemente, California, for $180 a month. I think it goes for a bit more today."

"From the start, the creating of the shows was a totally collaborative effort," Paul said. "First, there was our good friend and prolific writer, David Allen, who was a major contributor to *Sing Out '65*; singer-songwriter Kathe Green, daughter of celebrated composer John Green; Scottish folksinger Effie Galletly; and future actor Glenn Close, with whose father, Dr. Bill Close, we had worked in the Congo. Late in 1965, on our return from touring Japan and Korea, a talented young singer/song-writer from Santa Fe, New Mexico, Frank Fields, joined our writing corps. His songs quickly helped give our shows a contemporary edge. In 1966 at

Giving some direction to a cast in the 1960s.

Tennessee Tech in Cookeville, Tennessee we met Ken Ashby, Dick Smith, and their folk-rock group, the Volunteers. They dropped everything, came on the road, and started writing and performing their new songs in the show. That same year, two other gifted young writers from Tennessee started traveling with different casts: Cabot Wade, who immediately teamed up with Ken Ashby and Dick Smith, and Bill Cates, who was writing for Tree Publishing on Nashville's Music Row.

David Mackay helped organize musical operations and produced Up with People's albums for more than three decades.

"By the end of the '60s, with all the new writing input, the show had much more of a young rock feel. In 1970, writer-producer Bobby Scott ('He Ain't Heavy, He's My Brother' and 'Taste of Honey') produced a live album of an Up with People cast in concert in Tucson, Arizona. In 1972, we recorded another live album in Tacoma, Washington, with A&M Records' Hank Cicalo engineering and producing. About that time, Frank Fields and Dick Smith—along with bassist John Tracy, drummer Chuck Wansley, and guitarist Tim Murtaugh—started a band called the Smithfields. Buddha Records released a recording of their funky arrangement of the song 'Up With People.'

"In London, an Australian record producer, David Mackay, took the Smithfields into the studio and recorded some of Frank Fields' original material. David, who now has an impressive collection of gold and platinum albums to his credit, had just produced the New Seekers' international hit, 'I'd Like to Teach the World to Sing,' and would soon be producing Bonnie Tyler.

"For the next three decades, David Mackay would not only produce most of the Up with People albums but also would help organize our musical operation. Over the years, dozens of David's colleagues, writers, arrangers, and musicians have been involved in producing and teaching the shows. Two British musicians who participated in staging our shows in the early '70s became particularly successful in writing and producing hit records: Alan Tarney, with the Norwegian group Aha, and Terry Britten, who wrote and produced for Cliff Richard and Tina Turner.

"The writers David brought in to work with us included John Parr, cowriter of 'St. Elmo's Fire,' and Michel Mallory, one of France's most successful pop/rock song writers who cre-

Tom Sullivan's work with Paul and the Up with People creative group began in the 1970s.

ated most of the hits of megastar Johnny Hallyday, sometimes called the French Elvis Presley. David would bring all the writing and recording talent down to his home and studio south of London in the rolling hills of Surrey. We spent weeks at a time there throwing ideas around, writing, recording demos, and ultimately producing the finished product. All the Up with People creative team spent time there over the years: Herb, Ralph, Pat Murphy, Ken Ashby, Lynne Morris, Bill Welsh, and me.

"Wales supplied more talent per capita than any other country with writer Paul Carman; his music partner Peter King; Peter's wife, Lorraine; Sheila and Cheryl Parker, lovely vocalists in the true Welsh tradition; and well-known arranger Richard Coddle and his brother, bassist Lawrence. It was always fun doing sessions with the British musicians like brilliant guitarist Geoff Whitehorn, one of U.K.'s top studio musicians and for a time lead guitar for Bad Company. For hours on end, he would cheerfully and tirelessly tackle every musical challenge David threw at him so long as cups of tea kept coming. Cliff Hall, pianist extraordinaire and compulsive storyteller, was nonstop entertainment.

"Back in Tucson, Up with People rented a small house, the Casita, where we brainstormed, conducted an ongoing think tank, and did our creative work for more than ten years. Blanton himself was part of the process. We'd frequently get together with him to talk about what was going on in the world and throw ideas around. He had a unique perspective on things, and we turned several of his comments into songs for the show. We sought ideas from all over the world. Two major contributors from Africa were John Kagaruki, record producer and artist manager from Tanzania, and Yawo Attivor, a musician from Togo. Song ideas came from anywhere. The *Frontline* special on PBS, 'The Romeo and Juliet of Sarajevo,' was the basis for our song, 'Last Embrace.' A journalist and author from South Africa,

With Pope Paul VI in Rome.

Derek Gill, coined a phrase regarding the conflict in Ireland that became the song 'Give the Children Back Their Childhood.' The comments of Up with People board member and astronaut Eugene Cernan inspired the song 'Moon Rider.' Other groups and artists such as The New Seekers, Cilla Black, Cliff Richard, and Gene Cotton performed some of our songs.

"In 1993 when Up with People moved its offices from Tucson to Denver, I thought it was time for me to pass the torch to the next generation. Herb Allen had already handed

his baton as music director to his longtime associate Bill Welsh. The obvious choice for the job was my good friend and music collaborator Pat Murphy. He had been an integral and indispensable part of the creative team with Herb, Ralph, Ken Ashby, and Lynne Morris since 1983, and Pat had all the qualifications personally and professionally. He came to our staging in Burlington, Vermont in 1972, an African-American bass player just out of high school in Philadelphia. The next year, he joined our music staff on the road. Two years later, with Ken Ashby and other UWP alumni, Pat formed the pop/rock R&B band Arizona with David Mackay producing. They signed with RCA Records and while pursuing their recording career took time to write a significant amount of material for the Up with People shows. When Arizona disbanded, Ken Ashby worked with us as a consultant and eventually became vice president of production. Pat was hired as a full-time writer.

"Our shows didn't always get rave reviews. It was easy for critics to dismiss us with the 'squeaky-clean' label. Of course, the students in the program were no different from any cross-section of young people you'd find on any college campus anywhere in the world. The difference was that they were excited about the chance they had during their year on the road to do something to help their fellow human beings. It was always a privilege for us to write songs that might represent their best aspirations and to expand their understanding of the world. I have to admit that, occasionally, our writing could seem a bit overly hopeful and optimistic. Some reacted adversely to this, but others derived hope not necessarily from the songs but from seeing young people from different races and cultures working together.

"Studies show that there is such a thing as the 'biology of hope' and that a certain level of hope is essential to human survival. But that's another discussion. We always tried to introduce an element of reality into our material, to qualify hopefulness, and to ask questions. We made statements about the human condition, about human rights, about hate and war, about poverty, and about needing to find our common humanity. We wrote a lot about the environment. There was one song in particular about the hole in the ozone layer called 'Hole in the Sky.' One of our board members who was an executive in the automobile industry objected to it, but to his credit did not press the issue and allowed us our artistic freedom.

"Sometimes, the more serious social comment we made in our songs might have been lost in the overall youthful energy of the performance. But ultimately, that spirit and energy were what it was all about."

~

The twenty thousand cast members from sixty-plus countries who traveled during Up with People's first forty years could suggest a never-ending list of highlights: playing for athletes in Munich after the terrorist attack in 1972; in the bullring at Madrid; for popes; in Watts and Carnegie Hall and the Hollywood Bowl; in Moscow and Beijing; at Royal Albert Hall; in Northern Ireland, Morocco, and Jordan; for astronauts; for students at West Point,

Up with People casts performed in a variety of venues, such as here on the steps of a cathedral in New York City.

"In Poland's 'longest village,'" Paul said, "we had a flat tire, and it seemed that the entire population came out to help us fix it. (That's me bending over as if I were helping.)"

Annapolis, and the Air Force Academy; for kings and queens and princesses; at presidential inaugurations; and in the barrios and inner cities of the United States. Their memories might include rolling into a Midwest town in a convoy of buses; missing the bus in Barcelona; and striking stage sets at midnight.

The first chance to make a dent in the iron curtain appeared early in Up with People's history. "To those of us who were in on the program in the '60s," Ralph said, "it seemed an impossible dream that we might one day penetrate that brutal ideological and physical barrier splitting the world. Ever a visionary, Blanton made it a practice of announcing to students entering the program each year that very soon they would be in Moscow, Warsaw, Beijing, Beirut, Jerusalem, Havana, and Johannesburg. There was always a shout of excitement in response, but also a feeling that reality would prevail, and that their tours would take them mostly to Omaha and Peoria and, hopefully, Brussels and Stockholm."

The initial break came in 1974 with a tour to Yugoslavia, a communist country with an independent bent. There was then little cultural exchange between the West and the Eastern bloc, so there was an air of great excitement when it was announced that the first cast to go behind the "curtain" would land in Zagreb in late October for a three-week tour.

Ralph was then in charge of all Up with People's shows, and Allen was the company's music director. The two worked with cast manager Jerry Shelsta to help the young performers learn several folk songs and key phrases in the Serbo-Croatian language to use in song introductions. Ralph and his wife, Debbie, accompanied the tour.

"After a sold-out show in Zagreb, we headed to Pula in Slovenia and then down the stunningly beautiful Adriatic coast to perform in Zadar, Split, and Dubrovnik—each an incredible mix of ancient and modern. Alongside the roads winding through the lush Croatian countryside, we saw walls and sections of buildings dating back to Roman times used now to complete barns and lean-tos. From Dubrovnik, we headed inland to Sarajevo and then to Belgrade. Audience response proved there was a great hunger in the East for contact with the rest of the world, and that the time had come to push hard to open more doors."

Two years later, in 1976, another cast made an even more extensive Yugoslavian tour. When it ended, the company embarked on a train that carried them north out of the Balkans through Austria and Czechoslovakia to Poland. Paul and his wife, Catalina, joined them there.

Blanton Belk with cast members in 1982. From Up with People's inception in 1965, Belk was central to the program's direction and growth. By the start of the 21st century, more than 20,000 young people from sixty-five countries had participated, staying as guests in the homes of 500,000 host families around the world.

"Cati and I flew into Warsaw in late May to link up with the cast that had just arrived by train from Yugoslavia. This was our first venture into a Soviet bloc country. We were there at the invitation of Pagart, Poland's official booking agency, and their top promoter, Jurek Romanski. Jurek, a very 'unofficial' and gregarious individual and incredible host, had hammered out all the details of the visit with Norwegian Hans Magnus, Up with People's vice president for Europe.

"This was a three-week, six-city tour. There were a lot of outdoor shows with young audiences and a rock concert atmosphere. At one point one of Poland's popular rock bands, Partiet, performed with us. The response to our show was wild, and you had the feeling that Up with People was created for such a moment, making a connection between two worlds artificially separated by ideology and politics.

"As the person who was responsible for pulling together the conceptual aspects of our shows and coordinating the writing, I knew this experience would impact future productions, and I wanted to soak it all up. Cati and I rented a car and explored the countryside, the villages, the cities from Warsaw to Zakopane in the Carpathian Mountains. This fascinating country of Copernicus, Chopin, and Pope John Paul II, which had been marched over for centuries by armies from the east and the west, is stunningly beautiful, and its people possess an extraordinary resilience and strength of spirit.

"Driving through the fertile farmlands in 1976 was like a step back in time—the neatly stacked hay, the old horse plows (there were also a few tractors), families traveling down the road in old wooden carts, the small wood-frame farmhouses with the intricately carved trim, the wedding celebrations with young and old in national costume. In Poland's 'longest village,' we had a flat tire, and it seemed that the entire population came out to help us fix it. On Sundays, the whole country was out on the roads walking to church—certainly a symbol of a unifying national faith but also a statement of a nation's culture and independent spirit.

"We went with the cast to see Old Warsaw, which had been rebuilt brick by brick after the Second World War. The most sobering and chilling experience of all was our visit to Auschwitz. We walked through its paths and barracks, by the crematoriums and gas chambers in silence, both out of respect for the victims and because we were struck speechless by the unimaginable suffering and human cruelty they represented.

"The cast performed on Poland's heavily guarded western border. As we looked across the Oder River into East Germany, I felt as if I were looking across the iron curtain. Our young guides were very outspoken about their situation and openly critical of their regime. They did not hide their contempt for Russia, their old nemesis and current de facto occupying power. They rejected the label 'communist,' preferring to be considered 'socialist' instead. You had the feeling that they were trapped in a geopolitical predicament, and it is no surprise that the Solidarity movement was born in that country's heart and spirit.

"A lot of people have claimed credit for ending the cold war, not least of all certain Western politicians. There were, no doubt, internal and external economic factors. Some have suggested that it was rock 'n' roll music that brought down the Wall. Obviously, there is no one reason. But having toured Poland and watched the young people from around the world in the Up with People show come together with the Polish youth to celebrate their hopes and aspirations for the future through their music, I suspect that the rock 'n' argument has some merit to it."

There are thousands of stories that could be told, each with a significance of its own. Included here are some of them from the first Up with People tours in China and Russia. But the full story of those forty years is a story for a later book.

"Heart's Still Beating"
Paul Colwell and Herb Allen

Check the pulse of humanity,
Sometimes makes you despair,
Someone always being hurt somewhere,
And it isn't fair.
But there are those moments
When we forget who we think we are,
With our stripes, sickles and hammers,
Suns and crescents and stars.
We can't find a barrier anywhere,
Can't find the enemy we thought was there,
For a moment we can trust,
For a moment it's only us.

Search the face of humanity,
It often brings you to tears,
Makes you wonder what we're doing here,
Sometimes it isn't clear.
Then there are those moments
When we can open up our minds,
Stand shoulder to shoulder
When a life is on the line.
And one more lost to hostility
Becomes unthinkable insanity,
Under layers of ancient dust
We discover there's only us.

    The heart's still beating,
    The fire's still burning,
    We may be feeling
    That the wind is turning.
    And the pain is healing
    Though the memories may be long,
    The heart's still beating,
    The heart's still beating strong.

13

A Song for China

To the surprise of many, the signs along the road to the world's largest nation were not in Chinese or English, but Spanish.

In the mid-1970s, the odds against Up with People being invited to China were 100 to 1. Richard Nixon met with Mao Tse-tung in 1972, but there were no diplomatic relations between the two countries, and Up with People, Inc. although international in its composition, was a U.S.-based corporation.

In 1977, Up with People casts were touring in Mexico and Venezuela and were invited to Los Pinos, Mexico's historic presidential palace, to perform at a birthday celebration for Carmen Romano, the wife of President José López Portillo. The guest list included the country's elite, including Anthony Quinn, Paul's father-in-law.

For the occasion, Paul teamed up with Ken Ashby to write "El Puente" ("The Bridge"), describing Mexico and a vision of all people crossing a bridge that would unite them and lead them to a better future for the children. The audience was profoundly moved.

Paul sang the verses, which seemed logical, as he was the author. "But the other reason," he admitted, "was that I hadn't finished the song in time for the cast to learn more than the chorus."

One of the most affected by the song was the widow of Lázaro Cárdenas, Mexico's reformist president who had nationalized the Mexican assets of foreign oil companies. During the festivities following the show, she sought out Jose Antonio Rios, Up with People's coordinator for Latin America. "You should take this to China!" she exclaimed.

A champion of popular causes and a political activist, Cárdenas told Rios, who was Venezuelan, that she had good connections in the Chinese Embassy, and gave him names of people to talk with there. Rios consulted next day with

Up with People's tour of China in 1978 was the first of any international performing group since Mao's Cultural Revolution, and was expected to be a test case. At the Children's Palace in Shanghai, the children were enthralled.

Blanton Belk in Tucson, and soon was meeting with Chinese diplomats.

Those meetings and a subsequent flurry of consultations in Mexico City, Tucson, and Caracas led to an invitation six months later for a cast to visit China. Rios flew with Up with People Vice President Jack Hipps to make final arrangements at the Chinese Embassy. To be acceptable to the Chinese, in the absence of relations with the United States, this initiative had to be set up through Mexico with Rios, a Venezuelan, as the official leader of the delegation. The cast of thirty-five was completely multinational, with a sizable contingent from Mexico and other Latin American countries.

Hipps had been born in China, where his father taught at the University of Shanghai. The family had returned to America when Jack was fourteen. His memories of China and its people were deeply etched in his mind. Hipps' taped journal during the 1978 tour described the long-separated streams of East and West coming together. "One of the most significant aspects," he recorded, "was the instant communication established through the song Paul Colwell wrote with Herb Allen."

"Yao Tao-chung helped us create it," Paul said. "He was an archivist in the University of Arizona's Department of Music. His American friends called him Ted. We sat together in a small conference room at the Up with People offices on Campbell Avenue in Tucson. We'd come up with lyric concepts and then see how they would translate. Herb and I worked with a guitar and piano. We had an idea of the feel we wanted, the tempo and mood. We'd do a Western treatment of a Chinese five-note pentatonic scale, but not exactly. The theme was the Yangtze River, a symbol of the nation's identity. In English, the title translated as 'Our Friendship Deep and Long.'

"Ted Yao was an excellent poet and translated everything we expected to perform, then wrote the words in Chinese on large poster boards. Most songs required four of them. These would be our 'slide show,' held up by hand, to help audiences understand the lyrics of the songs."

Up with People would be the first multinational performing group to visit China in nearly forty years. "Some rock group had just been there, I think," Paul said, "and it was not a success. With us, they were being very careful. For instance, we would not be singing 'What Color is God's Skin?' since they maintained officially that God did not exist. We couldn't sing 'Moon Rider,' one of the hit songs of the show, which was about an astronaut in space seeing 'a world without any borders, without any fighting, without any fear.' Their media had carried little about America's space program, and they apparently weren't anxious to have us sing about it. Also, philosophically, conflict was essential to their ideology."

The company landed in Beijing on a China Airlines flight from Tokyo at noon on May 3, 1978. A very cosmopolitan Mr. Chang, who spoke impeccable English and was obviously the man in charge, escorted them into the city. Their rooms in the new wing of the old Beijing Hotel had sweeping views of gigantic Tiananmen Square and, in the distance, the Temple of Heaven.

"That evening," said Paul, "after a superb dinner, we were introduced to a Mr. Wang, who spoke no English or Spanish. He would lead the tour on behalf of the Chinese Association for Friendship with Foreign Countries, our sponsor. In diplomatic wording, Wang indicated that we would not be performing per se, to audiences in general. We knew that, of course; this was a 'tryout' engagement, like a show opening in Hartford to see if it could make it on Broadway."

The itinerary for the next three weeks was announced: Beijing, Nanjing, Hangzhou, Shanghai, Guilin, and Guangzhou. Beijing visits would include the Great Wall, the Summer Palace, and the National Conservatory of Music, where a performance was scheduled. The friendship association would give a banquet.

At almost every occasion where children were present, they performed for the visitors.

"At the Great Wall," Hipps said, "we were grouped for a photograph when a big crowd formed around us and the cast spontaneously began singing 'Tiananmen,' a popular song they'd learned. It took everyone by storm. It was a win with our sponsors, too, who had seemed nervous, but now started wearing our Up with People pins. We gave some to the kids who were visiting the Wall with their families."

On September 10, 1978, Jürg Kobler's historic photo of the cast in Tiananmen Square ran on the cover of *Family Weekly,* the predecessor to *USA Weekend*.

Hipps' first entry into his recorder was made on the balcony of his room, "where it won't be picked up by listening ears." He was hardly being paranoid. The Cultural Revolution had officially been over for less than a year, but the social tsunami it had created could not as easily be ended by decree.

"That night," Paul said, "we looked at the program we'd planned for the Conservatory of Music and made some cuts; each song had to be introduced by the translator, and we thought we'd go on too long. But the next morning, our hosts told us they didn't want us to leave out anything. Jack and I, with the text boards, were delegated to be the 'slide show!'"

"The conservatory visit had our hosts extremely uptight. They went over every lyric." Had the visitors been less naïve, they would have been as uptight as their hosts.

The day of the conservatory event began with a visit to Mao's Mausoleum in the huge Tiananmen Square. Thousands were already at the shrine when the cast arrived at 8:30. Lining up four abreast, the visitors walked into the entrance in absolute silence to face a giant statue of Mao, seated before an enormous tapestry of China. Then they filed past Mao's body, which lay in a glass vacuum in an adjoining room.

Swiss photographer Jürg Kobler, who traveled with the cast, sensed the significance of the moment; his photograph, with Latino cast members front and center and thousands of Chinese in the background looking on as they waited to enter the mausoleum, would later be carried across the United States on the cover of *Family Weekly*, the predecessor of *USA Weekend*.

At three in the afternoon, the company arrived at the National Conservatory of Music to find the entire student body awaiting them in the auditorium. To courteous applause, the visitors were shown to their seats. After a word of welcome, a program began that showcased outstanding artists ages fourteen to twenty. They displayed dazzling talent on the classical guitar, zither, piano, and violin. Male and female vocalists performed, and "Old Man River," in resonant basso profundo, was magnificently sung in Chinese.

"As one artist followed another," Paul recalled, "you could almost feel us sinking lower into our seats. Here we were, a group of mostly amateur youth from different countries, being overwhelmed by the finest talent of the largest country in the world, and then expected to go up onto that stage and give our show. I think more than a few of us were wondering, 'What have we gotten ourselves into?'"

"Well, we didn't know, but neither did they," said Hipps. "It was fascinating to watch. The show began with an upbeat choral number and choreography that had a lot of movement. Next came a piece with a sort of pop-rock feel. Both were applauded. Then Paul's song began, and immediately you could sense a collective intake of breath in the auditorium. First there was surprise, then delight, and then excitement. In English the lyrics say:

> We have come here from far away
> To bring you greetings
> Thank you for taking
> Such good care of us
>
> From the rice fields of Canton
> To the oil fields of Taching
> You can hear the people
> Singing their song of hope
>
> We're all on this earth
> And we share the same sun
> Though we speak different languages
> Our hearts beat the same
>
> Everybody come together
> To sing this song of friendship
> May our friendship be as deep and long
> As the Yangtze River

"Faces in the crowd just seemed to glow. From that moment on, the audience and the cast were absolutely connected."

"The response moved us," Paul said. "It really did. And it was a great relief to know the song accomplished what we hoped it would; it seemed to delight and touch them deeply."

"By the end of the show," said Hipps, "the audience was wildly and enthusiastically standing in a prolonged ovation. As the cast went out into the aisles, they continued to clap and just wouldn't stop."

A visit was scheduled for that same evening to the renowned Beijing Opera. The cast was running late, but the curtain was held for them. A visit the next day to the Summer Palace, with its enormous lake and six hundred acres of breathtaking beauty, impressed everyone. "In the dynastic era," Hipps said, "a person even looking at those areas could be beheaded. Now there were so many people there that it was almost claustrophobic!"

The guest list for the friendship association banquet the following day included the Mexican ambassador, a high-ranking official from the Ministry of Culture, and numerous senior people. In the planning for the event, politics took precedence.

"We had our first head-on with them," reported Hipps, "in that they asked Jose to respond to the toast, and he strongly indicated that he would not be the one to do this, that it should be Blanton as Up with People's president."

The discussion went on for some time, escalating higher and higher. The Chinese were adamant, saying that the Mexican ambassador was a close friend of Mrs. Cardenas, who had been their host in Mexico City, and so forth. Nothing Rios could say would make them change their minds. The return banquet, which Up with People would host the following day, "would be the time for Mr. Belk to speak," they said.

From the first day, the Chinese tour leaders had focused their attention on Rios; Mariacristina, his Italian wife; and Latin American members of the cast. They sought them out on the buses, and ate with them at meals. "You definitely feel the distance in relation to the North Americans," recorded Hipps. "Ideological rigidity like this is a paradox, of course, considering the response to Paul's song, as Paul is from the United States."

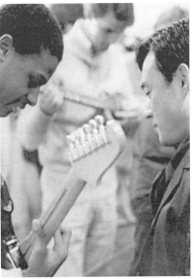

A cast member's guitar gets official scrutiny.

Toasts at the banquet that evening emphasized that the government was making a great effort to open up the country to foreign contact, and that because the Gang of Four had been dealt with, a group such as Up with People could experience China and exchange views. Mao's wife and three leftist intellectuals had radicalized the Cultural Revolution and become known as the Gang of Four. They were imprisoned a few months before Up

"The songs we expected to perform," Jack Hipps said, "were written in Chinese on large poster boards. Most songs required four of them. These would be our 'slide show,' held up by hand, to help audiences understand the lyrics." Hipps, here with a board, was born in China and spoke the language.

with People's visit, and Vice Premier Deng Xiaoping, against whom they had conspired, had been reinstated.

In the return banquet, Belk said that by the year 2000, when the world would be so much smaller, the most vital element would be human relations. Up with People would offer its services, he said, in bringing people from across the world together so each could understand the other. This was well received.

The conservatory's chancellor presented Colwell with an autographed copy of an out-of-print book of revolutionary songs. A prestigious composer, he had written a famous modern ballet, "The Detachment of Red Women."

On their final day in Beijing, the company was shown the Central Institute for National Minorities, where a concerted effort was being made to win and develop cadres from the country's fifty-five different nationalities. "Minorities make up only six percent of the population," Hipps noted, "but live on fifty percent of the land. That evening at our hotel, we called the cooks and waiters into the dining room to sing for them. It was the first uncontrolled situation we'd had, and it showed how deeply our music and the cast's spirit reach people. They were incredibly enthusiastic, and of course wanted to get down all the words and melody of Paul's song."

The party traveled from Beijing to Nanjing by overnight train. In Nanjing, a call to an official at the U.S. Liaison Office revealed that he had been cautioned by the Chinese to "cool it," and "not to try to do anything with us." He described as "amazing" what was taking place.

A traveling show from Shanghai provided a rare glimpse of some of the country's best puppeteers, who controlled their meter-tall figures by thin metal rods from below the stage. The performance opened with a brilliantly lit blowup of a handwritten poem by Mao and a choral number backed by a symphony orchestra. "There is no question but that music plays a giant part in this culture," Paul said. "People sing everywhere here."

Fathers of the revolution looked down on a responsive audience at the famed Conservatory of Music in Beijing.

At the Shanghai Conservatory, the cast performed for a wildly responsive audience. When the cast members moved into the aisles for a conga line number, the crowd cheered, shouted, pushed, and joined in. Colwell's song, Hipps noted, was again a sensation. "As was happening everywhere now, they asked for the music and the words. We had been advised prior to our visit that the people would not respond to direct interaction between the audience and the cast."

The next day they were taken to a commune, apparently a model one. It covered twenty square miles and had a population of 38,000, all organized into production teams. "It was very impressive, of course," Paul said. "Every vegetable looked like it had been hand-grown. In fact, it probably was."

"They're singing in Chinese!"

A few days later near Hangzhou, they would see a different picture. Passing a sign that read, "No Foreigners Allowed Without Special Permits," they entered a commune that specialized in growing silk. Villagers there did everything from mating the moths, producing the larva, and harvesting the cocoons to soaking the cocoons in water, unraveling the thread, putting it on the spools, and shipping it to the textile factories.

Children, often the focus of Paul's songs, were lined up to greet their visitors at the Children's Palace in Shanghai.

"This was the most authentic village we experienced," Hipps recorded, "dating back several hundred years. You felt you'd seen how 80 percent of China lives, practically at the subsistence level, but with enough to eat and clothes to wear, basic health conditions, and a place to live."

By contrast, in Hangzhou the cast lived outside the city in a 1930s hotel on the shore of the fabled West Lake, traditionally a symbol of beauty in the Chinese culture. They were treated royally, given a cruise, and appropriately awed by an eighty-foot Buddha at a temple built around 300 AD.

Guangzhou was the last city on the tour. As the country's main international business center, it attracts five thousand buyers from fifty countries to twice a year trade fairs. "There seems to have been quite a hassle here between our guides and the local sponsors over whether we could perform," Hipps said. "It was obvious that the local people were resistant, and that our guides wanted very much to have the show at the conservatory or some appropriate place. The issue was resolved by a typical Chinese solution to a conflict: the conductor of the Pearl River Orchestra brought a string ensemble of twenty-five, plus soloists, to the hotel, where they performed for us, and we performed for them. Nobody lost face."

"A visit to Guangzhou University left an indelible impression and brought home to us the harsh reality of the Cultural Revolution," Paul said. "The institution had been closed for years, its professors sent to the countryside for work and re-education. The rector of the university was visibly excited to now be reopening. Witnessing major surgery at a local hospital using only acupuncture as anesthesia was another unforgettable and traumatic experience. We were deeply impressed with how tough the Chinese are. One doctor confided that they just didn't have the money for more modern forms of anesthesia."

On their final night in the country, the cast gave a closing banquet for the six hosts who had traveled with them and for local leaders of the friendship association. Just as the evening was ending, Paul stood up. He had purchased a *liu chin*, a small guitarlike four-string instrument, at a department store in Beijing. He proceeded to play "Blue Grass Ramble," to everyone's delight. Then he recited a poem.

Hello and goodbye.

"I hadn't really finished it, but by the end I did. I'd give one line, and Mr. Ching would translate it, and that gave me time to think about the next one. I listed all the wonderful sights we'd seen. It basically said, 'you've shown us your land, you've taken us to the Wall. But most of all you have opened a door.'" The next morning, the company left for Hong Kong.

"China was an incredible experience," Paul reflected. "To be there in a very brief window of time in the transition between two eras—of Mao and the Cultural Revolution, and modernization—made it all the more fascinating. There was a sense of newness, things opening up, great curiosity.

"As I left, I thought of the Chinese of antiquity who spent centuries building a wall to keep out their enemies. Now their descendants, our hosts and guides, had opened a door to us in three weeks. I also thought with much gratitude of the thirty-five young people in our group who opened so many hearts across that nation."

Six months later, on January 1, 1979, China and the United States established full diplomatic relations. In the fall of 1985, a cast of one hundred and fifty toured the country again. KUAT, the public television station in Tucson, sent a film crew on the tour. The program that resulted, which Ralph Colwell coproduced, was titled, "A Song for China." PBS carried the special in eighty-five U.S. markets.

CBS, in a national promotion for the 1986 Super Bowl, ran a colorful clip of an Up with People cast rehearsing for that year's halftime show in a snowstorm at the Great Wall.

On the last day of the tour, Paul Colwell said to their Chinese hosts, "You've shown us your land, you've taken us to the Wall. But most of all you have opened a door.'"

Can We Sing a Song of Peace?

Paul and Ralph Colwell, Ken Ashby, Herb Allen

Can we sing a song of peace
In a world that's full of fear?
Can a melody of hope
Ever hope to dry a tear?
It's an easy thing to say,
But it's so hard to hear,
Will the fighting ever cease
If we sing a song of peace?

Can we sing a song of love
When we're hostages of hate?
Will it be heard above
The shouting at the gate?
Can we stop the sands of time,
Can we hold the hand of fate?
In this world of push and shove
Can we sing a song of love?

Clouds are gathering on the horizon,
And, on the wind, overtures of war,
It may be too late to settle for peace
If we wait till we've settled the score.

Can we sing a song of peace
When they're knocking down the doors?
Can you hold an olive branch
And hang on to what is yours?
Till the weapons that destroy
Go to join the dinosaurs,
Can there still be hope at least
If we sing a song of peace?

14

Can We Sing a Song of Peace in the USSR?

On the final night of the Moscow performances in Russia's premier auditorium, the audience demanded encore after encore.

Paul Colwell and Herb Allen set out for the Soviet Union via the library of the University of Arizona in Tucson. There, for days, they submerged themselves in a sea of Russian proverbs. They were searching for the essence of a song.

"People who know Russia say there is a proverb there for almost everything," Paul said. After searching through thousands of them, he decided to write a song about someone going to Russia to find one.

It was 1988, a year before Poland would hold its first free elections since World War II and the people of East Germany would beat down the Berlin Wall. Up with People was about to make its first visit to the Soviet Union, the first of any multinational performing group since the cold war had begun.

By1988, Up with People had an established international presence. In addition to annual tours in Western Europe, North America, and Latin America plus a sixteen-city tour in Japan in 1986, casts had visited Yugoslavia in 1974, Morocco in '75, Poland in '76 and '77, China in 1978 and '85, Jordan in '84, and Australia in that same year, 1988.

"I doubt there was any cast member since Up with People began in the 1960s," Paul said, "who hadn't heard Blanton Belk say, 'Someday you'll be in China and Russia.' What had been a goal and intriguing vision for years would soon become a reality."

The cold war was beginning to thaw. But perestroika, Mikhail Gorbachev's program of social restructuring, was less than twenty-four months old, and in the West, understanding of the Soviet Union was spotty at best. Anne-Cecilie Kaltenborn, a twenty-year-old student from Oslo, told of some reactions from the cast's host families about the impending visit. "Poor things," one mother had lamented. "Do you have to go?" "It must be a terrible blow to you on your tour," said another.

Of course, the opposite was true. The overwhelming feeling was one of excitement and anticipation. Up with People had been working for years to arrange the visit, knowing that the opening of the iron curtain was a critical component in bringing the world together. This visit, the first of any multinational performing group, could be a significant step.

Up with People's longstanding language guru and corporate secretary was Dr. Marshall Cartledge. Cartledge put Paul and Herb in touch with a student at the University of California, San Diego. "Her name was Tanya Wolfson, an émigré from Leningrad, " Paul said. "She ended up translating all our songs into Russian for slide projection during the show. And she helped us write 'Poslovitsa,' which means 'Proverb' in English. Herb and I would have a line or thought for a verse, and we'd give it to Tanya by phone or fax. She'd return it to us in Russian, we'd see how it might work, and make suggestions. We went back and forth like that for weeks. We wanted the song to be amusing, heartwarming, and memorable, and, above all, to make sense. 'Poslovitsa' told of a stranger coming to Russia in search of a proverb, and the people welcoming him to their homes and having fun with him. 'You don't find your proverb by looking somewhere else for it,' says the song, 'it's right there in front of you.'"

Three cities were on the two-week schedule: St. Petersburg (then called Leningrad), Kalinin (which has since reclaimed its ancient name, Tver), and Moscow. The seventy-five-member cast, which represented fifteen countries, had toured for eight months in the United States, then in Norway, Sweden, and Finland. In a mild, sun-washed springtime in early May, they arrived in the small Finnish town of Lappeenranta, some eighty kilometers from the Soviet border. They would stage their show at a local school building. They would learn "Moscow Nights," a beloved Russian song and rather satirical piece written by the foremost semi-underground poet Vladimir Vysotsky. They would also learn to introduce all the numbers in the show in Russian and, of course, learn "Poslovitsa."

In the pleasant environment of the Finnish town, Anne-Cecilie made a comment that reflected one of the ironies of the time. "They are so close to us, but still so far away. We're only an hour away here, but I know that the moment we cross the border, we'll be in another world."

There was never a lack of
enthusiasm in the Russian
audiences.

Paul advised band members to have their acoustic instruments always with them. "You need to be ready to perform at any time." On the bus trip to the border, the cast kept practicing the chorus of "Up with People" in Russian.

Hans Magnus, Up with People's vice president for Europe, was primarily responsible for arranging the visit. He traveled to Moscow numerous times to meet with representatives of Sputnik, the country's official youth travel organization, who were to be the company's hosts. His principal contact in Russia was Sergei Yastrebkov. (Hans and Sergei became close friends during this time, a friendship that would grow even closer during Up with People's three subsequent visits to the Soviet Union. Sergei would travel to Western Europe and the United States to familiarize himself with the Up with People program.)

In the Soviet capital, Hans found an air of excitement about the coming visit, mixed with apprehension; there was simply no precedent for this kind of show or this kind of tour. On departure day from Lappeenranta, Magnus said, "there is a mood of exhilaration, expectation, and uncertainty of what lies ahead for the coming two weeks. After a forty-five-minute drive we arrive at the Finnish border, where passports and visas are checked by Finnish customs. The video team that joined us last night is having problems, as their permits were

Against the familiar backdrop of the Kremlin towers, the cast is photographed in Red Square. Mary Hart (center), popular host of *Entertainment Tonight,* flew from the U.S. to take part in Up with People's Moscow shows.

not in order. Ralph will be in charge of this group on the tour. We leave the Finnish border after about half an hour, and are driving into no-man's land. All the students on the bus are quiet as we sight our first Russian checkpoint. The busses are flagged down by two young soldiers, and a senior officer boards, checks the passports, counts the passengers, writes the number into the driver's passport, and then waives us on. After another ten minutes we arrive at the main border. Everyone has to leave the buses with their luggage, and go through a passport and baggage check. We had been told that all of our luggage would be searched. Two hours later we re-board the buses, roll into the Soviet Union, and then go through one more guard station."

At the small town of Viborg, Ralph said, "We pull into a small parking lot where we link up with Tanja and Ilena, who will be two of our guides. We walk with them to have lunch in a large restaurant, and have there what is probably the quietest meal any Up with People cast has ever experienced. Nobody speaks. Everyone just looks around at the waiters, the buildings, at the people walking outside, realizing we are actually in the Soviet Union."

While the bus drivers were obtaining some special insurance, someone produced a basketball and a game began. "A few cast members start singing, and before we know it we are in the midst of our first impromptu performance in the Soviet Union," Ralph said. "People are looking out of the windows, gathering around, breaking into applause as the cast sings 'Up with People' in Russian. Somehow, this first informal encounter in a Viborg parking lot breaks the ice, establishes contact with Russians, and the cast begins to relax. As we drive on, we wave good-bye to the first friends we made in the Soviet Union, and the country seems less frightening than some anticipated when we crossed the border a few hours ago."

Four hours later, the convoy reached Leningrad (St. Petersburg). "We are immediately overwhelmed by this most beautiful city. We pass palaces, ancient churches, and majestic buildings in all shades of yellow, orange, and red, down wide streets alongside statues of Lenin. At the huge Hotel Sovietskaya, we get our first traditional welcome, which would be repeated many times during the next weeks. As the cast gathers on the steps, a little girl, beautifully dressed in a national costume, comes forward with a piece of bread and salt and hands it over with the official greeting of Leningrad. On behalf of the cast, Hans receives the bread, expresses our gratitude for the welcome, and our excitement of being in Leningrad and the Soviet Union."

"At dinner that evening we meet with Sputnik officials," Paul recalled. "Our first impression is that we are going to be working with young people. I think all our hosts are between twenty-five and thirty-five years old, and they are very enthusiastic. We are given a sumptuous meal, and go over the program for the next three days."

Ralph then met Alexij, who was in charge of the video group and their program. At the end of the meal, the cast sang 'Up with People' in Russian. "I finally get to bed around 1:30 a.m.," said Magnus. "I look out the window over Leningrad, and it seems almost unreal that the first day in the Soviet Union is already behind us."

After Hans and others finally turned in, Paul, with unquenchable curiosity, strolled the streets in the dim glow of the famous "white nights" of late June. He managed an hour of sleep before sunrise at 4:00 a.m.

Day two: "In the morning we visit the Leningrad Memorial," Ralph said. "We're told that during the nine-hundred-day Siege of Leningrad from 1941 to 1944, more Russians died here than the total number of British and American soldiers killed during the entire Second World War. A million starved to death. At the memorial, Katrina, a German girl, and a young American lay a wreath. 'I will never forget,' Katrina says later, 'being a German in Leningrad, and knowing the suffering my country had caused this city, and then being asked to lay down a wreath at the memorial. It was one of the most difficult things that I have ever done.' She is deeply moved when a Russian veteran of the siege speaks a few words to her in German. 'He seems to have forgiven everything that happened,' she says.

"We go to the Hermitage, or Winter Palace, once the home of the Russian tsars. The guide tells us that if we spend one minute at each exhibit, it would take eight years around the clock to see everything. We understand something of the wealth and power of the tsar as background for the revolution.

"Day three: At a children's hospital the children sing for us and then learn 'Up with People' in Russian. Each wears the bright red neckerchief of the Pioneers. At a visit to a park, a dozen children surround each cast member. There are more than that around Ross, who draws images in the sand to explain his name; the children fascinated with a black American who is deaf."

"After lunch, we rehearse for our first public show in the Soviet Union," Hans said. "At curtain time the hall is packed. I've been asked to introduce the show, and there is applause when I speak of building a more peaceful world. I go to the back of the audience, and then into the overflow crowd outside the theater. Suddenly I find the doors behind me are locked! Finally, I convince a policeman who I am and gain entrance, after a desperate moment of fear that I would miss Up with People's first performance in the country. From the opening number, there is an electric atmosphere in the auditorium. The words of the songs are projected in Russian on a screen. 'Can We Sing a Song of Peace?' takes on a new meaning tonight. At the intermission more people must have been allowed in, as they are standing ten deep up against the stage. The rock 'n' roll sequence gets a wild response. 'What Color is God's Skin?' is heard in silence, which after a moment is followed by thunderous applause. Finally, we get to Paul's 'Proverb' song and it is an immediate hit. The audience laughs, applauds, and demands encores. Encore follows encore. Dimitrij comes on stage with flowers for the cast and thank-yous from Sputnik. We leave the stage and he turns to me to say, 'We have never seen anything like this. It's a tremendous hit. Congratulations.' Sergei, who took the risk to bring us here, comes up from the audience with tears in his eyes and says, 'This is fantastic. You have touched our hearts. There's all the response of a rock concert but really quite different, because your show is all about human emotions.'

"Ralph, Paul and I go for interviews with Leningrad Radio and Izvestia, the national newspaper. The interviewers ask when we can return and if Soviet youth will be able to travel with us. Later we meet Igor Granoff, the promoter for our Moscow shows, who has traveled to Leningrad for the performance. He is full of compliments, and says that in Moscow we will be in the largest hall in the Soviet Union, where music superstar Billy Joel performed, and that five

Soviet groups will be on the program with us. Dimitrij says he has heard reports from every place in Leningrad we visited that people were deeply impressed with the cast and what they represent. Even the Intourist bus driver who took a group to the Children's Hospital called to say that had he realized who he was driving, he would have been much more helpful. At the end of the evening Sergei takes me aside to say, 'You have touched us profoundly. From the first time I met you and Steve [Up with People Vice President Steve Woods] in Moscow, I knew your group was different. We need this.'"

There is a memorable moment during a visit to the venerable Leningrad Conservatory of Music with Tim Clark, an African-American from Omaha, Nebraska. Paul said: "This conservatory produced some of the 'giants' of Russian music. Tim has a music degree and is an exceptional vocalist, compared by some to Lou Rawls. After a tour of the facility, the conservatory director gathers all the students to listen to Tim sing several pieces. One is a stirring rendition of an old spiritual. It is very moving to see Tim perform in that historic setting—for him a dream come true. The students, recognizing legitimate talent, give him a rousing ovation."

On the bus to Kalinin next day, Ralph and Hans had an interesting discussion with Sergei about Stalin, Soviet history, and the hope perestroika sparked in younger people. "We in the West can hardly imagine what they must now feel living in a country that has endured dictatorship for generations," Hans said. "'Much is changing here,' Sergei tells us, 'but it will take a long time before the fear of authority goes out of us.'

"In Kalinin, we are again given the traditional welcome. In the evening Paul, Ralph, and I have dinner with the local director of Sputnik, Natasha, and the director of Komsomol (the young communist league) to go through the program. After dinner, we walk to the central post office, which is the only place in this city of half a million from which long-distance calls can be made. Reed Thompson, our show director, tries to call back to Tucson, but is told it will take several hours. He finally gets through at 3 a.m., but nobody answers.

"A 'Peace Wave' program is to be put on by Komsomol the next day, and we are scheduled to participate. The street is crowded, and we join the informal folk dancing. What a sight—stout Russian women grabbing some of our students, both black and white, and, arm in arm, singing and dancing in the streets.

We split up onto three stages erected in different locations for the celebrations. A cast member teaches 'Up with People' to several hundred, who join in the choruses with us. Instant communication. Everyone is amazed that the songs are all introduced in Russian. After press interviews, I ask the director of Komsomol if she has been satisfied. 'No,' she says, and I'm surprised. Then she continues: 'Without you, this whole event would have been a flop. I'm very happy you are here because you saved the day. But I'm not happy that we cannot do something like this on our own.'"

A boat trip on the Volga the following day included many local young people. That night, Sergei, Ralph, Reed, and Hans went over the program for Moscow, including the arrival of Mary Hart, the popular host of *Entertainment Tonight*, who was flying in to appear with the cast.

The show that night was standing room only. The audience responded with waves of applause. Encores were demanded for "Poslovitsa." Just before the final curtain, people rushed to the stage to give flowers to the cast, and an unscheduled encore show was announced for the following afternoon. It too was packed.

"You can see in people's faces," Paul said, "that there has never been anything like this in the Soviet Union. I met an old soldier, a veteran of World War II. In Russia, they wear decorations of heroism on their everyday attire, and this man had many on his worn, dark gray coat. 'Thank you for bringing the grandchildren of the people I fought against,' he said. 'Tell the world we want peace, and thank you for coming here.'"

In the evening, cast members were invited to visit families across the city. "Hans, Reed, and I go with Natasha to the apartment of one of her friends," Ralph said. "It is a typical residence for a single person, twenty by twenty feet. Good food and champagne are served, and the discussion ranges far and wide. Our hostess has a guitar and I sing some songs and we present our gifts.

"Walking home in the early morning, Natasha tells us about the phone call she got from a member of the Central Communist Party in the Kalinin region, who told her what a moving experience it had been to see the show. We get back to the hotel just as cast members return from all different directions with their Russian hosts, taking emotional farewells, and hearing cast members say that this was the most incredible experience they had ever had, just sitting around the dining room tables of ordinary Russian families, talking about their lives, their countries, and the future. One had asked the family what perestroika meant, and the mother answered, 'It means that you are here in my home, that we talk, and that we don't need to worry about it.'"

On the first day in Moscow, the towers of

Glasnost and perestroika personified.

the Kremlin presented an impressive sight. Hans said: "We lay flowers at the grave of the unknown soldier, surrounded by tourists speaking every language imaginable. The Red Square has been closed off, except for a long line of people going right across it and into Lenin's Mausoleum. Police are everywhere. All cameras are taken away from us. Guards and police closely watch us, check everyone carefully, and line us up by twos. Amazingly, Ralph's video crew has been let into the Square, and they film the cast. The guards are even grimmer as we enter the tomb, this 'most holy place' for the Soviet people. The cast is photographed in the square afterwards. I think many of the cast members probably do not realize what a historic picture this really is.

"The next morning I go with the cast to the Pioneer Palace, a Moscow showcase for tourists, then for a CBS interview and in the evening a TV appearance with producer Igor Granoff on *Moscow Tonight*, a program seen in most of the country. We broadcast from the seventeenth floor of the studio, which is enormous, like everything else in the Soviet Union. Granoff was one of the country's first pop performers and handled the entertainment during the recent summit. He is promoting our show, and then organizing a large festival following our visit. After the broadcast he takes Paul, Ralph, Reed, and me for dinner in a marvelous restaurant, with champagne, caviar, and much talk about Up with People.

Hans Magnus receives the traditional welcome of bread and salt, this time on a stage.

"Mary Hart arrives the next morning, which is a Friday, and goes with forty of the cast to the Peace Palace for a discussion with the Soviet Peace Committee. Two young men are the hosts, and apologize that we are not able to use the main hall, as the country's top educators are meeting there today. We have the chance to ask many questions. They are frank and open in explaining problems left over from the Stalinist and subsequent eras, the difficulties of perestroika, and the stress of the people needing more than they have right now.

"Just as we are leaving, a few teachers from the educators' conference are on a break, and ask who we are. We explain that we're an educational program and ask if they'd like us to sing. They go away for a few minutes, and before we know it, we're in a large conference room in front of fifty of the leading educators of the Soviet Union. We explain our program briefly, our hopes for an exchange, and then sing a few songs. The response of this distinguished group is enormous. One woman says, 'We will welcome you back to the Soviet Union, and if you give us the words of your songs, we will have children all over the country singing your music the next time you come.' Teachers surround us, asking how they can keep in touch and work out programs for the future."

Sputnik gave a farewell banquet in the evening, as the cast was to perform on Saturday and Sunday, the final two days of the tour. "The banquet is at

Slovanski Bazaar, a popular restaurant close to Red Square," Paul said. "Mary is seated next to Sergei, our principal host, and Alexander, also from Sputnik. She has made an impression! There are talks and toasts and tributes, and eventually Sergei sums up the courage to ask Mary to dance, which draws laughter from other Sputnik friends, who don't quite dare to do the same. At the end of the evening, the cast surrounds our table and sings 'Poslovitsa.'"

Showtime. Granoff and the Moscow theater designers created an innovative dual-stage setting, with a colorful logo at the back depicting both Sputnik and Up with People. The performance is to open with a small dance group, and then the cast will appear in an ensemble with Russian performers in a song Granoff wrote written for the occasion. Next, five Russian groups will perform, followed by Up with People as the finale.

"At the green room before the show, Sergei and his wife and son appear," Hans said. "He is full of compliments. Mary Hart tells how she is enjoying her time with the cast, and looking forward to her first Up with People show. We have no idea how many will come. The tickets have only been on sale for a week. By curtain time, ten thousand are in the hall. The show begins and we think the Russian performing groups are very good, but they get a tepid response. After an hour and twenty minutes, it is our turn, and the atmosphere changes almost at once. The crowd is quickly 'into' the show, and Ralph's video crew records an historic performance. Once more there are encores of 'Poslovitsa,' and in the finale, Mary Hart is front and center, arm-in-arm with the Soviet groups and the cast reprising 'Poslovitsa,' and then 'Moscow Nights.'"

On Sunday morning, Magnus, Paul, and Ralph, drafted a memo for Sputnik as a basis for discussion of future tours and Russian participation in the casts. After lunch, they headed to Red Square for pictures. They set up in front to St. Basil's Cathedral at the end of the square, attracting considerable attention, but the police left them alone once they learned who they were.

After the photo session, Sergei said he had been in touch with the Ministry of Education about Soviet students spending a year with Up with People, beginning the following spring. Magnus proposed a meeting somewhere in Europe to work out the details.

"Sergei gives me a big embrace and then with tears in his eyes quickly turns around and walks out of the hotel. I feel at this point that though we may be far

Up with People's
Moscow shows were
presented in the Olimpiski
Arena, one of the largest
in the USSR. The crowd
jammed up against the
footlights.

apart politically and live in two very different systems, there is a real bond of friendship between us now. We can build on this to bring our two worlds closer together," Magnus said.

The worlds would come closer in the following years as Russian students joined companies touring internationally, and casts toured ten Soviet cities under the sponsorship of the Union of Russian Theaters. In 1989, Ralph and Herb were with an Up with People cast that made a three-week tour of Ukraine. Ralph coordinated the filming of the visit by Lenfilm, one of the country's top movie studios. The one-hour special was broadcast nationally on Soviet television in 1990. During a brief three-cast tour of Leningrad and Tallinn, Estonia, in 1990, cast members were allowed to live with host families for the first time. Many families willingly moved out of their own rooms to accommodate the guests. One company then split off to visit Leipzig in East Germany and another paid a return visit to Poland to play in the Union Hall of the Gdansk shipyard where Solidarity was born.

The Soviet tour in 1991 included Gorky, Russia's fourth-largest city, off limits to foreigners since World War II. Not even diplomats had been allowed there. That year, Gorky's name was changed to Nizhny Novgorod, and the performances of Up with People, with cast members representing nineteen countries, became the city's first window to the outside world in nearly half a century.

Twelve thousand people attended the final Moscow show. Alexi Krupin, who was in charge of the lighting for the show, invited Paul, Ralph, and Mary to visit his home for a late-night snack. The video crew went along and filmed Paul, Ralph, Mary, and Alexi and his wife, Farida, a psychologist, talking about their lives and their countries. Farida looked around at the faces in the room, and then said to Paul, "You don't have to look very far for a proverb."

"Till I Fell in Love with You"
Steve and Lynn Colwell

Sailing alone on the ocean of life,
Drifting along with the tide,
What is the meaning?
Not sure what I'm feeling,
Just going along for the ride.
What is the chance
A smile or a glance
Could make this lonely heart pound,
Turning everyday words into poetry
And my whole world upside down?

> *I never knew the meaning of life,*
> *Never believed that dreams could come true,*
> *I never knew that time stood still,*
> *Till I fell in love with you.*

I learned all the words to the song of life,
But I just couldn't sing the tune.
Something was missing, like a cold winter's night
Empty of stars and of moon.
Then like a puzzle that comes together,
Suddenly the picture is whole.
Now the moon and stars are there,
'Cause I found a mate for my soul.

> *I never knew the meaning of life,*
> *Never believed that dreams could come true,*
> *I never knew that time stood still,*
> *Till I fell in love with you.*

15

FOUR WEDDINGS
AND A FUTURE

The love life of musicians in the limelight is typically a subject of inter-est, especially when it develops in not-so-typical ways.

The four men were dedicated to their calling, and while their hearts and hormones spoke to them as loudly as anyone's, they resolutely attempted to keep their focus on their work. But circumstances in the mid 1950s turned Herb's thinking in a new direction. He had operated overseas for eight years, and by then was probably as much at home in Sicily or Sussex as in Seattle. With Bill Bauman and a few others, he'd returned to the United States on a freighter from Europe. In early February 1955, he was meeting maritime workers at Sault Sainte Marie in Northern Michigan. Herb had just received a message, and he was excited.

"I'd known a young lady named Jane Becker since I landed in Europe in 1948. She is a gifted musician, and we often worked together playing two-piano inci-dental music for shows. I liked Jane a lot, but then I liked all girls. I had no romantic notions at that time.

"When I went to Italy in 1950, Jane went to South Africa with her father and two younger brothers. I was in a Milan restaurant in 1952 when a friend came in with the news that Jane's father had been killed in a plane crash in the moun-tains of the African Cameroons. I remember saying to myself at the

Herb Allen proposed to Jane Becker by mail in 1952. To the maestro's delight, she answered "yes" by transatlantic call.

time, 'I think I'm going to look after that girl.' I was in Italy and she was thousands of miles away in Africa, but the thought was clear. As I recognized the love growing in my heart, I knew what I wanted the future to be.

"I didn't see Jane for six months after that. When we did meet, and I opened my mouth to speak, nothing came out! She continued working in Europe, and for the next two years we were frequently in the same place. Fortunately, my ability to speak had returned, although I never outright told her what I was feeling. But I'm no good at hiding things, so what's the difference? Dr. Buchman gave me a prod that day in Sault Sainte Marie with a note that read, 'Faint heart never won fair lady!'

"I wrote proposing to Jane on February 3, which, unknown to me, was the anniversary of her father's death, and she got the letter three days later in Switzerland, very fast for mail in those days. She phoned me right away from where she was living, in a chalet above Lake Geneva. It was a terrible phone connection, and I couldn't hear her well at all. She seemed to be muttering something.

"'What?' I asked. 'What was that?'

"She said something again and I still couldn't get it.

"'Jane, I can't really hear you.'

"Well, then she yelled so loud into the phone that people there said you could hear her all over the Alps! 'Yes! With all my heart!'

"'Holy crow!' I replied. It was one of my more gallant responses. At that time, Jane was taking care of the son and daughter of friends who were working in Italy, so she couldn't come to the United States for two weeks. When she told the little boy what was happening, he said, 'Oh, poo on Herbie.'"

As newlyweds, the Allens were on the premiere tour of *The Crowning Experience*, a musical based on the life of pioneering black educator, Mary McLeod Bethune. It starred Muriel Smith, who had created the role of Carmen Jones on Broadway and in London sang *Carmen* and played for five years in *South Pacific* and *The King and I*. *The Crowning Experience* opened in January 1958 in Atlanta, Georgia, the first show in history presented there to black and white audiences who were offered equal seating. Allen collaborated on the show with George Fraser and John Hopcraft and wrote the music for "There's Always Room for One More," one of its most memorable songs. *The Crowning Experience* ran for five months in Atlanta, and then broke all records in the 123-year history of the National Theater in Washington, D.C. Allen conducted the orchestra.

~

The Colwell brothers' mother, True, once confided to a friend her concern that her sons would never have time to get married. Then, between 1967 and 69, all four were wed. Then True worried that with the demands of their schedules, it might be a long time before there would be grandchildren. Within the next five years, each son and his wife had three children.

When Paul Sr. died in 1997, a month short of his ninetieth birthday, there were several great-grandchildren. By the time True passed away in 2004 at ninety-five, she had thirteen great-grandchildren, with a fourteenth on the way.

Two days after True's memorial service, the brothers, their wives, and several of their sons and daughters and spouses were at a restaurant in the foothills of Tucson's Santa Catalina Mountains. There was much reminiscing, of course, and laughter, and eventually the topic turned to how the four couples had met, become engaged, and married. Recalling the event later, Steve said, "Because we had been touring continuously for so many years, some of our stories were pretty unconventional."

Ted said he and Mary had begun their relationship more "normally" than the others. "We fell for each other during Up with People's beginnings. She was a lovely, athletic New Zealander, and, fortunately for me, the attraction was mutual. But then she went off to college and I went into the Army. We got engaged just before I shipped out to Vietnam, where I served as an artillery officer. We were married in San Marino in 1969."

"I well remember the first time I saw Cati Quinn," Paul said. "It was in June of 1961 when she stepped out of a car at the Caux conference center in Switzerland. Steve, Ralph, and I just happened to be standing outside the building, and let's just say the girl was noticeable. We were introduced to her there on the sidewalk."

Tall, slim, with long black hair and a dark olive complexion, Catalina Quinn was the daughter of Anthony Quinn, the actor. She had arrived in Switzerland with her mother, Katherine, whose father

Paul and Cati, 1969

(Top) Paul and Cati in 2005 at Vashon Island in Seattle's Puget Sound.

(Bottom) Ralph and Debbie in Thailand in 2005, traveling with an Up with People cast that gave benefit performances to aid victims of the devastating tsunami that hit the country the year before.

was film producer Cecil B. DeMille. In the fall of that year, the Colwells, Herb, Catalina, and a number of others accompanied a young Chinese troupe from Taiwan throughout western Europe with their stage drama, *The Dragon*. Then in the fall of 1962 and spring of 1963, the brothers, along with Catalina, toured the length and breadth of Italy with *The Condor*, a play about revolutionary students written and performed by young Latin Americans.

"Day in and day out, working in such close proximity, I often thought about Cati," said Paul, "but I generally deferred to Ralph when it came to girls. I was always competitive with him, yet in this department I figured he had the looks and everything else going for him, so I'd better let him go first. In spite of being so unsure of myself, which was compounded by my health struggles, I still persisted in dreaming about the possibilities."

Asthma had been a constant threat for Paul. "It was pretty bad in Europe. With advice from the doctors in Switzerland, we decided I ought to be in a warmer climate for a while. So, in the autumn of 1963, I decided to accept an invitation to go out to India to work with Rajmohan Gandhi. Gandhi was organizing a 'March on Wheels' through the country's major cities to focus the nation's attention on some of the social and moral issues that he felt were impeding India's political and economic progress."

Paul had expected the trip would be a break not only from cold weather, but also from his nonstop schedule of performing. He even left his instruments with Steve and Ralph, who worked that winter in Europe.

"The truth is my health wasn't much better in India than in Europe, and I ended up doing more music than ever. I played all the time. I had picked up an old guitar in Bombay. It was painted black and I never did figure out the make of it. It had a broken neck, so you could bend it and make the note waver. I remember singing in Telugu, Tamil, Bengali, and a couple of other languages. In Madras (now Chennai), I had the honor of performing for Rajagopalachari, Rajmohan's maternal grandfather and India's first governor general after independence. He was a highly venerated elder statesman. Cati was on that trip, and that's when I fell deeply in love with her.

"There was a big conference coming up in a few weeks in a mountainside center under construction at a place called Panchgani just outside of Poona. In addition to helping oversee crews of students working on the project, my assignment was to enlist five hundred musicians, songwriters, and singers to assist Rajmohan Gandhi's nationwide

Ralph and Debbie's courtship took place during a tour of Italy with 135 other cast members.

campaign. Well, I not only didn't get five hundred; I didn't get even one. What I do remember is putting on songwriting classes with Herb out in a cow pasture in the Ooticamund tea country there in South India."

Three years later, Paul was in Fort Myers, Florida, with the cast of *Sing Out '66*. "That's where I asked Cati to marry me. Her answer was that she would think about it. All right, I figured, that would be OK. I imagined one of her considerations would be that I was seven and a half years older than her, and we had never really got to know each other except in 'working conditions,' so to speak. Two weeks later, when we were at Fort Bragg, North Carolina she asked to see me. I held my breath. She told me then that she didn't feel it was right. I still held my breath. When I could breathe again, I answered that I didn't agree, that I still believed it was right, and that I still had the same feelings. But I said I would respect her wishes. That night we had a show to do, and I was dying."

Mary, Cati, Debbie, and Lynn; Colwell brides and brides-to-be in Uruguay.

By that summer three *Sing Out* casts were in operation, and they met in Estes Park, Colorado, high in the Rockies, to stage a new production. "Cati had come there from Panama, where she had been doing PR for the shows. I hadn't seen her for a while, and when she was there right in front of me, I realized I was more in love with her than ever. She was really dedicated, and a very spiritual person, always has been. Her parents had divorced and I knew that was hard for her. During those weeks and months, I got a lot of

In Rajmohan Ghandi's "March on Wheels," elephants sometimes led the parade. During the nationwide tour Paul fell in love with Catalina Quinn.

help from good friends. They could see that I was just a novice in this department. The following January, with a big-brotherly nudge from Blanton, I took Cati out on a dinner date. Around the end of that month, we were in Palm Springs doing a show for President Eisenhower. I learned that Cati was planning to leave the next morning to be with her father in Rome.

"I called her then, and said, 'How about taking a walk?' We drove out to Joshua Tree National Monument, which was about an hour away. There, among the Joshua trees and rocks and beautiful high desert scenery, I asked her again to marry me.

"'You don't know what you'd be getting into, Paul,' she answered. " You just don't know.'

"On February 14, Valentine's Day, right after we'd had that talk, the cast flew to Hawaii. Cati and I sat together on the plane, and a flight attendant came and brought us champagne. We hadn't officially announced our engagement yet. But that did it. The cork was now out of the bottle, so to speak. Four months later, in June, we were married in the beautiful garden of Cati's mother's home in Connecticut."

Things moved faster for Ralph. During a weekend in 1967 when the physicist Buckminster Fuller came to visit Up with People casts in Texas, Ralph "noticed" Debbie Cornell.

"I found myself looking at her a lot, but I didn't let her know I was looking. Later, I found out she wondered why I didn't say hello any more. I think now that keeping my distance was partly an echo of being so single-minded in the past, but mainly, I was just shy." Ralph remembered meeting Debbie when he and his brothers performed at her school, Sidwell Friends, in Washington, D.C. She was eleven and he was seventeen.

Twelve years later, the age difference no longer mattered, although other things did. "I couldn't really say I had fallen in love with Debbie because we'd known each other only at a distance. She was smart, an accomplished cook, and an expert seamstress; brown eyes, raven hair, a classic beauty. And who was I? Just a guy from California, a musician, and a country musician at that! Would she have me? What if she said no?

"In January of 1968, Debbie was in California and I was on the East Coast. I wanted to propose, but not over the telephone. With a couple of her friends, we set up some kind of ruse claiming that she was urgently needed in New York for a special event. She decided to catch a redeye that night. Well, Debbie isn't taken in by ruses; she knew something was up. When she arrived at JFK early in the morning, I was there to meet her.

"I was really apprehensive, waiting for her to get off the plane. But when she emerged from the Jetway, all at once I felt a sort of epiphany; I knew this was meant to be. Debbie didn't seem very surprised that I was meeting her. My plan was to pop the question over breakfast at JFK, but every restaurant in the airport was closed! So, we got in the car and headed for Connecticut where she would be staying. I hadn't any Plan B, so I seized the moment; I proposed as we were zipping along the Van Wyck Expressway. How romantic can you get?

"Debbie was ready with her response. She said she knew she was going to marry me. Most women know. Guys are clueless. She told me she could, of course, wait and answer me later, but since she was going to say yes eventually, yes it was. You know, it was almost too easy. I think a good courtship helps make a good marriage. We really missed that, did things sort of in reverse, and had a lot to work out. Debbie said to me on several occasions, 'I married you, Ralph, not the Colwell Brothers!'"

In the same week that Ralph and Debbie were married in New York, their cast gave a well-reviewed performance to a packed out Carnegie Hall. At their wedding reception, Steve caught the bride's bouquet!

Debbie and Ralph's courtship took place during a February and March tour of Italy with 135 other members of their cast. If the trip were seen as a musical, with leaning towers and moonlight gondola rides, the theme song would certainly have been "Getting to Know You." Bus rides between show engagements gave the couple chances to talk on every subject that could be considered, or risked, at that stage in their relationship.

The company finished its tour and flew back to the United States in April. During an impossibly active week in May in which they gave a well-reviewed show to a packed Carnegie Hall, Ralph and Debbie were married in historic St. Bartholomew's Church on Park Avenue. "At the reception following the wedding," Ralph said, "there was one truly unique highlight. Steve caught the bride's bouquet!"

At the time of Ralph and Debbie's wedding, Steve had taken some friendly ribbing about being the oldest, the leader, the responsible one—and still single! It was time for him to take action.

"In 1966, we'd just finished a show in Colorado Springs when I heard about this girl with a five-string banjo coming to join the cast. I was excited about that because my favorite instrument is the five-string banjo, one of the trademark instruments of bluegrass music. When Lynn Hutner arrived backstage and opened her case, I was disappointed by what I saw—a four-string guitar. But I was far from disappointed in her. This effervescent five-foot two-inch, blue-eyed, Rollins College graduate dove head first into many aspects of Up with People, from solos in the show to public relations. We worked together, but alas, always at arm's length. Once we were interviewed together for the Italian press, speaking our best broken Italian. Slowly over the next two years, what had caught my eye now grabbed my heart, and I began to have the feeling there should be ten strings strumming together now, her four and the six strings on my guitar."

True Colwell, in her nineties, with her four sons.

The day after Ralph and Debbie's wedding, Paul drove Steve to a phone booth at a nearby golf course where they could have a little privacy. Paul walked over to a practice putting green. "He was hitting putts while I was calling Lynn," Steve said.

"I woke her up. She was in Europe, in Belgium at that moment, doing PR for an upcoming tour, and I don't think I'd calculated the time very well because it was 6:00 a.m. her time.

"'Hi, Lynn, this is Steve,' I said.

"'Steve who?'

"Well, how many Steves did she know? Of course she wasn't expecting any call at that time of the morning, not one from the other side of the Atlantic, and certainly not one from me. When we did get our identities clear, she figured I was calling to say that she was needed in another town, or maybe should do something with the show. Instead, I asked her to marry me. There was a long silence.

"After a few minutes of conversation that I don't really remember now, she told me she'd have to think about it. She'd be coming back to the States soon and we would have time to talk. It turned out that it was several weeks before she could get free, because she was needed to set up the tour."

When Lynn eventually returned with others from her cast, the conference at Fort Slocum was under way. The travelers were expected on the afternoon ferry and Steve was standing expectantly at the dock. Passengers disembarked, but Lynn was not among them. Another ferry docked ninety minutes later. Still no Lynn. Then the last ferry of the day came—and went.

Lynn Hutner said "yes" to Steve in 1968 on a walk in a park in Lima, Peru.

By 2006 they had four grandchildren.

"If you painted a picture—Norman Rockwell could do a good one—there'd be this guy standing on the dock with wilting flowers and a very sad expression. I didn't really think she wasn't ever going to turn up, because someone would have told me. But of course you wonder whether she'd decided to back out. You wonder what happened to her. Is she OK? It turned out that she'd stopped off in New York to visit a friend, and didn't arrive on the island until the next day. And then I wasn't at the dock."

When they eventually managed to get together, Steve suggested to Lynn that becoming engaged would be the best way they could get to know each other. "I told her that if it didn't work out for her, we didn't have to get married. So she accepted."

The next autumn, Sears sponsored a tour through Latin American countries, and a cast performed in cities where the company had a major presence. That tour was the last time the three Colwells performed as the lead group in an Up with People show. Cati joined the company in the second week of the tour. Steve, Paul, and Ralph, with wives and fiancées, were all together. So was Mary Caughey, who had just become engaged to brother Ted, then serving as a second lieutenant in Vietnam. In Argentina, they appeared on the country's most popular TV show, performed in major cities, and recorded an album in Spanish. From there, they toured Uruguay, Peru, Colombia, Venezuela, and Panama. In Peru, during a walk in a park in Lima, Lynn gave Steve the answer he was hoping for. Someone dubbed the trip the "Colwell Honeymoon Tour."

Herb and Jane, a creative team for more than half a century.

After a special performance in Washington, D.C., in January, Lynn and Steve flew back to Los Angeles for their wedding. It was the rainy season in Southern California, and an enormous tent had been erected for a garden reception. The night before the wedding, a violent storm hit. The tent was unceremoniously blown into an adjacent ravine. Fortunately, the nearby Beverly Hills Hotel was able to accommodate the party. A year and half later, Christopher was born and became the youngest member of Steve and Lynn's Up with People cast, traveling with his parents until the age of two.

"""

Paul and Ralph Colwell, Herb Allen
(Based on the words of Captain Eugene A. Cernan,
the last man to walk on the moon)

I can see the white of snow-capped mountains,
The blues and turquoise of the oceans blend,
Australia and Asia coming 'round the corner,
And I can't tell where one country starts
And the other one ends.

The sun is setting on the Pacific,
They're just getting up in Rome.
I don't see the lights of my city,
All I can see is home.

I know this view won't last forever,
Soon I'll be back to reality.
But isn't it the way we perceive things
That makes them what they will be?

    I see the world without any borders,
    Without any fighting,
    Without any fear.
    So, Captain, give the order,
    We're going to cross the next frontier.

THE VIEW FROM NOW

The Colwell brothers and Herb Allen have four different perspectives on the story of their lives. But their associates see a common theme. Some expressed it in an Orlando, Florida ballroom at the start of the new millennium.

It was the third day of Up with People's thirty-fifth reunion, in the first year of the twenty-first century. People from across the world had gathered for the event. They represented the nearly twenty-thousand

Fifty years later…

individuals from sixty countries who had been part of Up with People's extraordinary odyssey: millions of miles traveled; half a million host families embraced; millions of lives impacted by a song, a word, or a touch.

The program opened with a big-screen multimedia presentation, created by the sponsor of the morning, Toyota of North America. At the request of the reunion staff, the brothers and Allen, introduced to the crowd as Up with People's "creative founders," gave a half-hour concert of songs that traced their journey: They started with "Freight Train Blues," from their bluegrass/country roots, sung in 1965 during Up with People's first year; alums from that era were delighted as ever when Steve "stuck" on a high note. Next came "Pays de Coeur," written for a tour with the Belgian National Symphony during the country's 150th anniversary; then came "Song for China," "Vive le Congo!" and "El Puente."

The crowd stood and cheered, but before the four could leave the stage, their instruments were whisked away and they were seated on tall stools around a

"Herb still hasn't given up hope that one day we might become legitimate musicians."

piano to hear a choral medley of music they had composed. Then songwriter Pat Murphy bounced onstage and conjured up thirty-five guitarists for a riotous rap about the brothers' 1965 cross-country road trip, "... in a Pontiac station wagon packed to the roof with instruments, when they wrote that song called 'Up with People'—three words that made some serious history, and they've never told us who said them first."

They probably never will. The Colwells and Allen have been a "group" since the mid-twentieth century, and one of their secrets of working together is never to hog the credits.

Their quest, from the beginning, has been to bring the roads of humankind together. As to their story, each has a singular view:

Herb: "We all know it's true, that it's difficult to evaluate our own lives and particularly the effect we have on others. There is so much to be thankful for. To put it as simply as I know (and I'm a simple guy), I thank God for my parents, Mom particularly, who gave me a faith in God. Unshakeable. Inconvenient at times when I'm tempted to go in other directions.

"I'm thankful for my lifetime partner, Jane. Besides being one of the most intelligent human beings alive, she's quite a dish. So I keep my eye on her. I'm thankful too for our beautiful daughters Maryanne and Mardi, and their children, Adam, Joshua, Paige, and Hayley.

"I think of two things my mentors drilled into me: George Fraser said, 'Herb, make every song a great occasion.' I kept that in my mind when working with the casts of Up with People. The other key thought was, 'Music will never satisfy you. It's merely a "pencil in your hand" through which you can express your reason for being.'

"That 'reason for being' was vividly brought home to me during Up with People's visit to the Ukraine in 1989. Jane and I had been invited to accompany the cast; I would perform on the xylophone. We were both deeply moved by what we saw happening every night during the tour. As always, subtitles of the lyrics were shown on a large screen during the show. But the audience watched and listened with astonishment, some with their jaws agape, as those young performers 'connected' with them across the proscenium. I was more fascinated by the audience than by the show itself. Their faces seemed to ask, 'Can people really be as free and open as this?' In our larger stadium performances, the local militia just couldn't contain the crowds who poured onto the field during our high-energy numbers because they were so keen to participate. Almost daily during the tour I performed Rimsky-Korsakov's 'The Flight of the Bumblebee,' accompanied by our Up with People band.

"As Ralph so rightly expressed earlier on, the credit for any successes we've had lies with others. Thousands of others, in fact. Like my colleagues, I love people and I love music. The combination continues to be useful. That we were privileged for a time to carry the spark that helped to light the torch I believe is also credible. Let it keep on burning, please God!"

~

Steve: "Lynn and I were having an evening in the home of Vere James, one of the ex-Navy servicemen who took Paul, Ralph, and me boating on Lake Geneva way back in 1953. Naturally, we were sharing war stories. Vere asked me at dinner, 'Looking back, are you sorry now you didn't return home and pursue your music career?'

"'No,' I answered without hesitation. I didn't see how any amount of money or fame (as if we might ever have achieved either) could have been more fulfilling and exciting than pursuing a noble quest and using music to do it.

"Once we made the decision to be part of it, it was like we were being carried along by a giant wave, something almost beyond our control, that plopped

At Big Mama's Karaoke Café in Seymour, Tennessee, in 2003, Allen and the Colwells videotaped a live performance and made their first studio recording in over thirty years.

us down on the shores of Mackinac Island in the mid sixties, where we caught a new wave. How lucky, providential really, that we were at the right place at the right time.

"We'd set out as idealistic youngsters, one not old enough to vote, with revolutionary zeal to change the world. Then as 'old men' of around thirty, maybe mellowing a bit, but never losing our passion to make a difference, we joined hands with a new generation in writing and performing, and that carried us into a new dimension.

"There's no question we live in troubling times of war and suffering, and, perhaps worst of all, of national, political and religious polarization. Some claim we're doomed, heading for a black hole of extinction because humans and their nation states will always be controlled by baser basic instincts of greed, hate and fear.

"Maybe I'm too stubborn to abandon my youthful idealism or maybe I'm simply naïve, but I'll always believe that the best in people can win the day. What I've experienced is that it is possible for roads to come together as people overcome the frailties of their natures and embrace their strengths.

"Paul wrote a poem for the original Up with People show that spoke of a divine spark in all people. I believe that spark exists in everyone and that fundamentally all want a better future for their children.

"Will my grandchildren, Zoe, Evan, Finley, and Ella inherit a world where one culture, religion, or country has forced its way on others? Or can cultures and countries learn to work together for the benefit of mankind? That is a noble quest. Perhaps that is why we are here. I will never lose hope that such a change is possible.

"There is nothing about which I'm happier and prouder than to have helped bring into this world and raised with my wonderful partner three unique human beings—Chris, Corey, and Chip, who later married three very special people, Lisa, Ryan, and Sam.

"What a ride it's been and what a joy to have worked with, traveled with and raised families with my best friends—my brothers.

~

Paul: "We are not celebrities. We are not rock stars with any big hits to our credit, except for our song, 'Vive le Congo,' which climbed the charts in the Congo in 1960, and of course, 'Up with People,' which has gained a fairly wide grassroots recognition.

"It is by no means certain that the Colwell Brothers would have reached star status in the commercial music field had we continued on that course in the 1950s. We were not brilliant vocally or instrumentally, though our harmonies were pretty tight. Perhaps we had a certain teenage brotherly charm and chemistry working for us that carried into our adult years.

"It is a kind of Forrest Gump-like scenario, but because of our affiliation with MRA early on, a lot more explanation is required. Like Forrest Gump, we just happened to show up in the darndest places when events of historic significance were taking place—singing for one of the 'architects' of the European Union, performing in Tokyo for Prime Minister Kishi as he embarked on his 'reconciliation' tour of Asia, being featured at the Independence celebrations in the Congo, jogging and singing through China right after the Cultural Revolution, walking in India with Gandhi colleague Vinoba Bhave as he collected land for the landless, taking our Up with People show to the USSR just before the "Wall" came down.

On the lawn of the recording studio in Seymour.

"For us it was clearly a stroke of luck; three average guys hooking up with some people working on a very high level in hot spots around the world who offered us the opportunity to use our music to make an immediate and positive impact. Their contention that 'if you want to change the world you need to start with yourself' carried a certain inescapable logic. The hook there was 'change the world.' The values and sense of social responsibility instilled in us by our parents plus our youthful idealism made us ripe for the picking. The endorsement and active involvement in this endeavor of statesmen and national leaders in many fields convinced us this was something big and important, and that the goal of changing the world was, in fact, achievable if enough influential people could be enlisted. We were in it for the long haul with our 'lives, fortunes, and sacred honor.' Interestingly enough, through the years we had many sincere communist/Marxist acquaintances whose total dedication to their revolution we could relate to. And the respect there was always mutual.

"We can't claim to have changed or 'remade' the world. But the world, and the times, 'they were a-changing,' and we were lucky to be out there in the middle of it. Our experience in almost sixty countries on six continents was an incredible training ground. In 1953, I was about to attend Occidental College to study international relations, languages, and political science. I got all that, only in a different classroom.

"As the tumultuous '60s unfolded and we started questioning the extreme demands we imposed on ourselves, some fascinating new opportunities emerged. From 1955 to 1964, we did not set foot on U.S. soil. On our return to America, I had the distinct feeling that we were arriving in yet another foreign country. The first time I entered a store, I tried to figure out how to phrase my questions so the salesperson would understand. Then I remembered, 'Hey, this is my country. I speak the language.' Of course, having been away for so long, we would never see our country in quite the same way again. We'd had the benefit of seeing ourselves for years through the eyes of others. From that perspective, we were not automatically the 'greatest country in the world,' as so many of our leaders frequently, immodestly, and publicly like to proclaim. We are certainly one of many, but what does that matter anyway?

"Ours is a very special country, and young, so our song for its bicentennial suggests, 'Two Hundred Years and Just a Baby.' It is historically and culturally unique, and for the moment the lone superpower. With our tremendous resources, diversity, creativity, generosity, and democratic system, we can do great good for humanity, and we have. That position of power can also go the other way. It's a delicate balance. I submit that this international and intercultural immersion that was so invaluable to us should be a requirement (a couple of years anyway) for anyone aspiring to public office. It could have a helpful effect on their worldview.

"The timing of our return to the United States was perfect, during that creative and volatile decade when music expressed the feeling of the times. Again it was our good fortune to be in the right place at the right time with the right people and to be part of the creation of Up with People. This was the opportunity we were looking for. We had been off the radar for so long as troubadours, minstrels, (and even buskers) in distant lands that it

Four brothers.

was stimulating to get back into a mainstream mix. Our specialty throughout those travels was writing special songs and ditties, often on the spot and in other languages, for people, countries, and occasions.

"Over the next decades, our song crafting evolved and hopefully improved. As songwriters, we have been fortunate to have an immediate outlet for our material through the Up with People shows. It is a benefit not many writers enjoy.

"In retrospect, what I'm most grateful for, next to my talented and beautiful wife and artist, Catalina; our son, Wade, and daughter, Sabina, and their wonderful families; and our son, Jeb, is to have had the chance to work with some of the genuinely nicest, most interesting, and gifted people in the world, and for their loyal and lasting friendship. Foremost of these would be Herb Allen, who has had to put up with us three musical 'illiterates' for fifty years plus. Up with People would not have happened without Herb. And Blanton and Betty Belk, with whom we've traveled so many miles from Mexico to Brussels to Beijing and back, will always have my utmost appreciation and admiration. They put our enterprise together and steered it through the years.

"Back in the early 1950s we were lying around in our parents' bedroom one morning when Dad, reflecting on our recent involvement in MRA, said, 'How did we get into this anyway?' Our eight-year-old brother Ted's response was immediate: 'How did we get into it? What I want to know is how do we get out of it?'

The Colwell clan
after True's memorial
"celebration" in 2005.
She was 95.

"Ted was too young to be part of our musical combo at the time, and when we left home to travel, his remark to our mother and dad was, 'They're rats and cheaters.' He would join us later in Europe, Africa, and Asia and would briefly become a local 'rock star' in Sri Lanka with his group, The Four Tune Tellers. In 1965 he helped to start the second cast of Up with People, then went on to distinguish himself in combat in Vietnam. On his return he pursued a medical career, and is now practicing obstetrics and gynecology in Idaho. We're proud of Ted, though we can take no credit for his accomplishments. It is always a highlight for us when Ted gets out his guitar and joins in with us on stage, the kid who wanted to know, 'How do we get out of it?' Well, we've been in it together in a lot of places, and we're lucky to be together still."

~

Ralph: "I've been fortunate, since I was all of ten years old, to have others close at hand with whom I could pursue an adventure, a calling, and a career. At times I wonder what tack my life would have taken without the presence and motivation of two talented older brothers; the vast array of truly interesting personalities we associated with through more than fifteen years with MRA; the unflagging dedication of Blanton Belk; the beautiful and brilliant dancer, choreographer, and teacher Lynne Morris; and, most importantly, the ultimate good fortune of Debbie Cornell agreeing to marry me and remain so for thirty-eight years, good fortune topped only by our three children, Kit, Clayton, and Fletcher, and their five children (and counting).

"Some people strike out on their own and thus make their mark in the world. They are the rebels, revolutionaries, inventors, and innovators

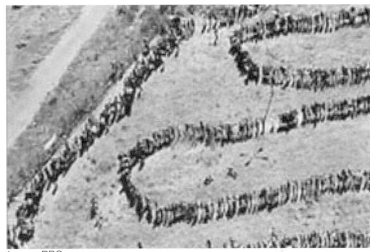

Image, BBC

who fly in the face of convention and shape the world according to their vision. Others take different routes, perhaps a bit less daring, but with the same desire and ability to see the world as it could be and ask, as Robert Kennedy did, 'Why not?'

On April 26, 1994, South Africans stood patiently for hours in thousands of queues across the country waiting to vote in their first democratic election. It marked the end of apartheid.

"It was only when Debbie and I decided to start a family, to finally break with life on the road after nearly twenty years, that I realized how much my life and to some degree my personality had been subordinate to the pressures and expectations of the larger group. I felt that on a personal level that I had ground to make up in being a fully functional, stand-on-your-own individual.

"What we treasure the most from those years is not where we were, but the people we were privileged to meet and get to know and, most of all, what we learned about the world. That is what I wish for every new generation of globetrotters, whether college students on study-abroad programs, a church mission, a stint with the Peace Corps, or simply biking the Pacific Rim. Make a lot of friends, but, more importantly, learn what makes the world go 'round and do something to help tip the geopolitical balance toward a safer, saner world. Sing a song; perform a dance; start a band; make a friend; appreciate the differences."

"The Day the People Came Together"

Paul and Ralph Colwell, Pat Murphy, Herb Allen
Written to honor South Africa's first free election, April 26, 1994

The old man was smiling,
Never thought he'd see the day.
So many people of all colors,
They raised a banner
That swept the barriers away.
And millions were dancing,
Farther than the eye could see.
They had been traveling a lifetime
Just to get there,
On the road to dignity.

> The day the people came together,
> A day that changed the world forever,
> In a thousand years they'll still remember
> The day the people came together.

On this day we will lay our weapons down,
On this day we'll stand on common ground,
A whole new journey is just beginning.

> The day the people came together,
> A day that changed the world forever,
> In a thousand years they'll still remember
> The day the people came together.

APPENDIX

"THE GREATEST MUSICIAN I KNOW"

In 2004, a thousand of Herb Allen's friends decided to tell him how he had influenced their lives. The occasion was the thirty-ninth annual reunion of Up with People in Tucson, Arizona. One morning, thirty minutes into a special concert featuring Allen, the Colwell Brothers, alumni, and local musicians, the tempo suddenly changed.

Paul Colwell said, "Oh, excuse me, Herb, there's something we forgot to tell you about." Allen's keyboard was suddenly whisked away. Jane, his wife of forty-five years, was invited on stage to sit beside him and, with his family in the audience, Herb was shown on a giant screen a multimedia presentation that illumined highlights of his life.

Dave Mackay flew to Arizona from London to pay tribute to Allen in 2004.

Colwell described how in Italy Allen had caught the imagination of a revolutionary poet who wrote songs for the communist leader Palmiro Togliatti. Blanton Belk had been in Italy's Po Valley in the 1950s when Allen had just received news of the death of his father. Herb, fluent in Italian, was scheduled to speak to a large gathering of rice workers. "I must do it," Herb had insisted. "Afterward," Belk recalled, "Madame Dosier, who led the workers union, was in floods of tears. 'I never thought I'd meet a young American with such a commitment,' she said."

David Grossman, vice president of Paramount Pictures and responsible for the company's music for television, said that Allen "allowed me to study under

Allen in Odessa in 1989, rehearsing a Ukrainian folk song with Russian hosts and sponsors before the evening's show. The stadium would be sold out, and militia attempting to prevent the audience from pouring onto the field would eventually give up and join the crowd.

him, and instilled in me a passion for music that would last a lifetime. Once he held a pen up just across my eyes.

"'What do you see?' he asked me.

"'Well, Herb,' I answered, 'to be honest, I don't see much. There's a pen in front of my eyes.'

"'Exactly!' Herb said, with his typical enthusiasm. 'The pen is your music. Your music is blinding you. And it will suffer if you don't get a broader idea of the people and the world around you.' Then he sent me off to purchase and read a volume entitled, *Sixteen Books That Changed The World.* It was about Thoreau, Einstein, Freud, and others. 'Let's talk about that the next time we get together,' he said.

"I was a drummer with the cast then and I was just seventeen. I'll never forget the moment during a rehearsal when Herb came over to my drum set and literally got down and put his head inside my bass drum. He listened to it as if it were the only instrument playing. Everything about the music had to be right. Thirty-one years later I still use what he taught me daily."

Grossman then presented Allen with Up with People's Lifetime Achievement Award.

Jill Johnson, who worked with major music organizations after her Up with People years, presented a tribute from Marilyn Bergman, president and chairman of the board of the American Society of Composers, Authors, and Publishers (ASCAP).

Up with People alum Craig Barna, conductor of major Broadway musicals, wrote in a tribute: "Every day of my twenty-five years in this business has been informed by this profound teacher."

Musicians, writers, arrangers, and producers from Britain who had worked with Allen sent video clips. Record producer David Mackay flew from London to pay tribute to "the greatest musician I know." In a video clip from Hollywood, film and TV personality Tom Sullivan said, "You've raised the consciousness of a planet."

Allen told the crowd, "I've still got tread on my tires, and you certainly have. Let's see what we can do now for the future."

MICHIGAN CONNECTIONS

Michigan, where Up with People was born, is the state where the Colwell family roots run deep. Sault Ste. Marie is forty-five miles north of Mackinac Island. It is the city where the brothers' great-great grandparents settled in the mid 1800s. Great-grandfather John Alonzo Colwell, one of Steve's namesakes, was a respected attorney and judge there. Among his clients were the Native Americans of the Ojibway Tribe. In the early 1900s, their maternal grandfather, Ralph K. Johnson, Ralph's namesake, was surgeon for a construction company engaged in widening the channel so the huge ore boats could pass through the St. Mary's River to the Soo Locks and on to Lake Superior. He was also doctor for the native population in the area, where he rode horseback to make his calls.

Four Michigan relatives fought with the Union Army in the Civil War—Great-grandfather Fayette Johnson, a captain who suffered wounds from which he never fully recovered; Great-grandfather Matthew Glenn, also a captain; Great-grandfather Stephen Colwell, Steve's other namesake, who ran away from home at the age of fourteen, too young to join as a regular and so became a drummer boy; and Dr. George K. Johnson, who was commissioned surgeon of the 1st Michigan Cavalry. He was also a mayor of Grand Rapids and witnessed the laying of the cornerstone of the University of Michigan, where five of the family later graduated. The brothers' father, Paul Sr., was president of the Beta Theta Pi fraternity there in 1929.

A paternal grandfather, Walter I. Colwell, one of Paul's namesakes, unfortunately passed up the chance to invest a few dollars in a one-cylinder engine that a fellow named Henry Ford was tinkering with in his barn down the street in Detroit. When the Great Depression hit, Walter and his wife lost everything, including their home.

Although most of the family in the early 1900s moved to Detroit, where some decades later the brothers were born, the Sault Ste. Marie area remained a favorite summer vacation spot. Judge Colwell built a cabin on nearby Sugar Island in the midst of beautiful pine and birch trees by the St. Mary's River. It still stands and is enjoyed today by extended family.

THE AMAZING
MUSIC HISTORY QUIZ

At the fortieth reunion of Up with People in Tucson, Arizona, in 2005, a somewhat whimsical quiz circulated among alumni. It listed "firsts" in the audacious adventures of the Colwell Brothers and Herb Allen, and held a few surprises even for those who knew them well:

Do you know:

1. Who was the twentieth century's youngest performing percussionist?
2. Who was the era's youngest orchestra conductor?
3. Who was with the first musical production to tour post-World War II Germany?
4. Who comprised the first big-city bluegrass band?
5. Who were the youngest trio contracted by a major record label?
6. Who were the first Western musicians invited to sing in an Asian parliament?
7. Who was in the first American musical group to have a thirty-seven language repertoire?
8. Who played in the most venues internationally of their generation?
9. Who performed in the most countries of anyone in their generation?
10. Who traveled the most miles of any musicians of their generation?
11. Who introduced Caribbean steel bands to North America?
12. Who set the Guinness World Record for continuous drumming?
13. Who created with others the second-longest running musical of the twentieth century?
14. What show set the all-time record for U.S. cities toured in a single year?
15. Who were the first non-African performers to tour Africa?
16. Who took the first international musical show to Eastern Europe in the 1970s?

17. Who took the first multinational musical group to China after the Cultural Revolution?

18. Who took the first international musical group to the Soviet Union in the 1980s?

19. Who invented, with others, the nonmarching band format of the Super Bowl halftime show?

20. Who wrote shows performed nine times with major symphonies and at seven World Fairs?

Answers

1. Herb Allen, age three, the world's youngest drummer, according to the *Seattle Post-Intelligencer*.

2. Herb Allen, age four, conducted the Seattle Baby Orchestra.

3. Herb Allen, age eighteen, was assistant music director of *The Good Road*.

4. Steve, Paul, and Ralph Colwell, ages fourteen, twelve, and ten in 1947, were labeled "Motor City Bluegrass Legends" by Eugene Chadbourne in *All-Music Guide*.

5. The Colwell Brothers, ages nineteen, seventeen, and fifteen, were contracted by Columbia Records in 1952.

6. The Colwell Brothers sang in the Japanese Diet in 1957.

7. The Colwells first sang in another lar.guage in Switzerland in 1953 for Robert Schuman, a founding father of the European Union, and eventually performed in thirty-seven languages and dialects.

8. The Colwell Brothers, in uncounted thousands of venues worldwide.

9. The Colwell Brothers performed in fifty-four countries.

10. The Colwells traveled farther than the Beatles and Elvis Presley combined.

11. Herb Allen in 1964 introduced the Steel Band of Trinidad and Tobago in a national tour.

12. Bob Quesnel, original drummer for *Sing Out '65*, played continuously for one hundred hours and twenty minutes in 1964 and made the Guinness Book of World Records.

13. Up with People's thirty-five-year run was second only to
    The Fantasticks, which closed in 2002.

14. In 1976, Up with People played in 771 U.S. cities to a total live
    audience of 3.9 million.

15. The Colwells performed 412 programs on Radio Congo in 1960 and
    toured the country with Up with People in 1968.

16. Up with People toured in Yugoslavia in 1974 and Poland in 1976
    and 1977.

17. Up with People toured in China in 1978 and 1985.

18. Up with People toured in the Soviet Union in 1988,'89, '90, and '91.

19. Up with People's production team. UWP performed in four Super
    Bowls in all: Super Bowls X, XIV, XVI, and XX.

20. The Colwells and Allen, with others. Symphonies: Up with People
    performed with Dallas, Denver, and the Boston Pops (twice each);
    Winnipeg; Belgian National Symphony; and the National
    Symphony, Washington, D.C. World's Fairs: Expo '67, Montreal;
    Expo '74, Spokane; World Expo '68, Brisbane; Expo '82, Knoxville;
    Expo '92, Seville, Spain; Expo 2005, Aichi, Japan.

Although only one of the above claims ever made the *Guinness Book of World
Records,* all the answers are believed to be true.

BIBLIOGRAPHY

Garth Lean – Frank Buchman: a Life (Constable, London, 1985)

Hansjorg Gareis – Stepping Stones (A German Biography, 1995)

Tom Sullivan and Derek Gill – If You Could See What I Hear (Harper and Row, 1975)

Dr. Morris Martin – Born To Live in the Future (Up with People, 1990)

Brian Boobbyer – Like a Cork Out of a Bottle (John Faber, 2004)

Warner Clark – Our World On Our Watch (Pooh Stix Press, 2005)

Norman Vincent Peale – Enthusiasm Makes the Difference (Fawcett Crest, 1967)

Jarvis Harriman – Matched Pair (Pooh Stix Press, 1999)

John G. Pribram – Horizons of Hope (An autobiography, 1991)

William T. Close – Ebola (Ivy Books, 1995) and A Doctor's Story (Ivy Book, 1994)

Charles Piguet – Freedom for Africa (Caux Edition, 1991)

Frederik Philips – 45 Years with Philips (Blanford Press, 1980)

Nelson Mandela – Long Walk to Freedom (Little Brown, 1994)

William Van Dusen Wishard – Between Two Ages (Xlibris, 2001)

Morris Martin – Always a Little Further (Elm Street Press, 2001)

Ian Baruma – Inventing Japan - 1853-1964 (Random House, 2003)

John and Denise Wood – Have Ocean, Will Travel (The Write Place, 2005)

INDEX

Frank McGee has built a distinguished career as a writer and journalist over half a century. In the tumultuous 1960s he covered stories as far afield as Brazil, Indonesia, and Viet Nam. As managing editor of *Pace* magazine, a contemporary of *Life*, *Look*, and *Holiday*, he worked with thought leaders from around the world.

During the 1970s McGee launched and edited *New Worlds*, the signature magazine of California's Orange Coast, and published a half-million circulation sports program for offshore power boat racing (*Bushmill's Grand Prix*). The University of California at Irvine tapped him to write the coffee table book commemorating the school's first twenty-five years. In the '80s and '90s he authored and edited books that were printed in a dozen languages.

From hundreds of letters and documents and scores of interviews, Frank McGee has brought to light the astounding story of *A Song for the World*. He lives with his wife, Helen, in Tucson, Arizona.

www.asongfortheworld.com